# THOUGHT LEADERSHIP

Edited by Stuart Duff

Published by:
Pearn Kandola Publishing
9400 Garsington Road
Oxford Business Park
Oxford
OX4 2HN

**Important guidelines for downloading worksheets from this publication.**
Permission is granted to photocopy the worksheet pages from the
iLEAD™ books or to download the worksheets free of charge from
www.pearnkandola.com. Only the original purchaser of this book may
photocopy or download the worksheets. To access the worksheets
online you will need to provide the ISBN number from the back cover
of your iLEAD™ book.

ISBN: 978-0-9562318-6-4

British Library Cataloguing in Publication Data
A Catalogue record for this book is available from the British Library.

Printed in Great Britain by Ashford Colour Press Ltd, Gosport, Hampshire

# ● CONTENTS

**List of contributors** (alphabetical)

| | | |
|---|---|---|
| Jon Atkins | Emma Kirk | Sally Rendall |
| Rob Barkworth | Stephan Lucks | Ceri Roderick |
| Sean Boyle | Joe MacAree | Paul Rose |
| Clíona Diggins | Ken McKenzie | Maraliese Spies |
| Polly Howard-De La Mare | James Meachin | Clair Thurgood |
| Holly Jones | Padraig Neary | Emma Trenier |
| Simi Jutla | Neil O'Brien | Maggie Van Den Heuval |
| Laura Haycock | Paula Philips | Louise Weston |

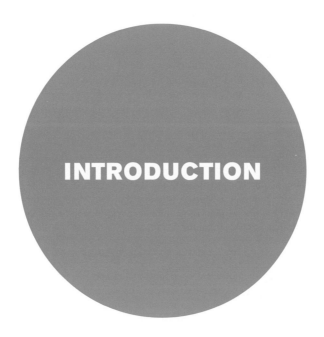

**INTRODUCTION**

This book is one of three in a series of leadership books based on the coaching experiences of Pearn Kandola Business Psychologists. Any manager aspiring to lead others will have a compelling interest in their own personal development. As coaches and experts in leadership skills, we have created iLEAD™, a series of three unique books based on the most important elements of business psychology.

Over the past thirty years we have coached leaders from hundreds of different organisations across all sectors. Using a combination of our own models and the best emerging research, we have helped those leaders to engage in change and further their development.

Now, for the first time, we have captured these models in three distinct books, one focused on people leadership, one on task leadership and one on thought leadership. Each book offers a chance for any manager to use some basic but essential psychology to help to improve and develop your approach.

## A Model of Leadership

Each iLEAD™ tool provides immediate insights and new ways of thinking about management and leadership challenges. There are also a range of interactive exercises to develop new understanding and practise new skills.

The iLEAD™ tools are based on our own strategic model of leadership, known as the Leadership Radar™. The model recognises that there are three core areas of leadership: People, Task and Thought. We use the analogy of a radar because leaders need to have an awareness of these three core areas to fulfil their role and be aware of where and how they use their time across each of the three areas.

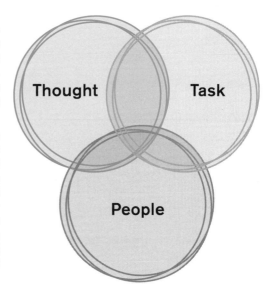

## People Leadership

The people leader inspires others towards achievement of ambitious goals through a combination of communication, influencing and engagement skills. They are openly passionate about what they aim to achieve, yet caring and considerate in the way that they approach others. They know that people are their most valuable resource and will do their utmost to secure and retain the commitment of their teams.

## Task Leadership

The task leader drives others towards achievement of ambitious goals through a combination of determination, resilience and clarity of focus. They take ultimate responsibility for the quality and delivery of results, and are highly skilled in the way that they delegate tasks and ensure that others are aware of the priority targets. They optimise performance and realise the full talents of the people around them in achieving results.

## Thought Leadership

The thought leader constantly looks to new opportunities and the future. They quickly evaluate complex and ambiguous situations and are ready to analyse and challenge tough decisions. The thought leader initiates changes and improvements, and is imaginative and open to taking entrepreneurial risk.

## Leadership Styles

There is clearly more than one way to lead. Leadership draws on a diversity of talent and resources, and the most effective leaders understand how to make the most of the situations and people around them. The keys to successful leadership therefore are self-awareness and the capacity to change. While we may at times understand the attributes of leadership, we can often struggle to demonstrate these at the times when they are most needed.

Our aim, therefore, is always to equip leaders with the skills they need, and more importantly to provide them with the motivation and desire to lead. The iLEAD™ tools address both of these challenges.

We hope you not only enjoy reading the tools, but also find ways to make immediate and practical use of them in your own approach to leadership.

# IMAGINING

# HOW TO DEVELOP STRATEGIC LONG-TERM GOALS

Understand what is involved in setting achievable goals and how to strategically plan for the long-term to avoid falling foul of biases.

## ● ISN'T IT INTERESTING?

Have you ever gone to the supermarket when hungry?

### Mmmm...

If so, once at home did you find a number of unusual items you had no intention of buying, such as doughnuts, pizzas with new toppings or delicious looking desserts, at the expense of basic foods such as bread, eggs, or potatoes? If this has happened to you, don't worry, you're not alone. It seems we find it notoriously difficult to delay our short-term needs or desires, for long-term requirements.[1] After a spontaneous shop (or maybe once we've eaten the offending items) we are struck by a bout of sudden guilt from the knowledge that we have indulged in purchasing unnecessary treats at the expense of our basic needs.

### Projection bias

Researchers[2] have proposed that this is where we are out of touch with our 'future emotional self' – that is, we find it hard to identify with predicting our future needs, because our current emotional state overrides these needs. This is known as the 'projection bias'. This happens despite us having experience of similar occasions (previous shops whilst hungry) and their undesirable consequences (lots of junk food and a serious lack of staples in the house). Simply put, projection bias means we ignore our long-term needs in favour of short-term gratification. However, if we are to learn to strategically predict our long-term needs we need to combat this bias.

In this example, we can start by not shopping when we are hungry, as this increases the likelihood of us buying only what we need. Mentally, this involves projecting our current emotional state (such as hunger) into the future to envisage how we are likely to feel (guilty if we buy treats and fulfilled if we stick to the plan). So when developing strategic long-term goals it is important to plan for the projection bias.

### This tool can help

Seeing a vision of the future is critical to planning a strategy and avoiding pitfalls like the projection bias. This tool is about **how to develop strategic long-term goals** and will help you to understand what is involved in setting achievable goals and how to strategically plan for the long-term to avoid falling foul of biases.

# ● STRATEGIC LONG-TERM GOAL SETTING

What about two years from now, or five? Ideas are all very well but making them happen is the thing. And then, how realistic is your idea, anyway? What happens if you kick off and then, eighteen months later it doesn't look so smart because, these days, the business environment, technology and all that seems to change from one quarter to the next – it's like being at sea, trying to sight land through a kaleidoscope.

Whether you're planning a long-term project, re-orientating a department or considering some diversification, it's about...

> 'Exploring the overarching objectives of the vision and translating these into clear, tangible actions'

...and contingency planning, in case it gets choppy.

There are so many books and articles on goal setting, but few of them give the basic requirements for a reasonable chance of success. So, even if some of it seems simplistic, we'll give you a better idea of the kind of thing you need to include in your long-term planning and some practical techniques.

Now, developing a concept and turning it into a strategy can seem like a daunting task. In theory you would probably want to have weeks or even months to sort out how you will build your vision. In practice this is not always realistic; however there are some straightforward steps that are useful to remember which can help to make it an easier and more enjoyable process.

To start, we've developed a simple model of the key features of developing and managing strategic, long-term goals below.

# ● V-SPORT – CREATE YOUR STRATEGY

The core elements of strategic goal setting are outlined below:

| Area | Description |
| --- | --- |
| V | **Vision** This is the strategy's focus. Ideally it should be in line with the organisation's ethos and complement overall goals and objectives. |
| S | **Stakeholders** Identify key customers, stakeholders and other appropriate parties to ensure their support. Keep them informed at each stage to maintain interest and commitment. |
| P | **Priorities** Prioritise what's essential to the strategy's eventual success – important once it's underway and time and resources are pressured. |
| O | **Opportunities** Keep everyone involved aware of the benefits being worked towards to help maintain momentum. Raise awareness, too, of smaller benefits resulting from the process itself – new skills training, opportunity for employees, increased awareness of competitor activity, etc. |
| R | **Risks** Take time to explore actual and potential de-railers and prepare ways of avoiding or managing them effectively. |
| T | **Timelines** Allow your strategy to be sufficiently flexible to accommodate changes within or outside the organisation. It is important to consider the current situation and future changes. |

The next section examines each of these aspects in more detail.

#  FOCUS FOR SUCCESS

Here are the key aspects of the V-SPORT model in greater detail:

## (V) ision

This is the cornerstone of the whole strategy and provides direction for the long-term goals. Putting this in writing to formalise it is extremely important. Ideally you should try to write this in a compelling, inspirational way as well as making it clear and transparent. People need to clearly understand – and identify with – the vision and direction.

Consider how this aligns with overall organisational goals and, as important, try to demonstrate that it contributes to individuals' personal and career goals, team goals and departmental goals. People are motivated by opportunities for personal development and if the strategy offers this you will gain commitment which, in turn, maintains momentum.

Consider the following questions to fully understand and build your own and others' commitment to your vision:

- What is your end goal?
- Why is this important to you?
- What are the implications of not achieving this outcome?
- What benefits will achieving this outcome bring to you/the organisation?

## (S) takeholders

It's important to consider the people who have some stake in the success of the strategy. This includes those who contribute to the initial vision statement, those who will have to be involved or will be affected at some stage of the process and those who will be affected by its outcome. Think about your audience and how you're going to explain the translation of the vision into actions. To do this, look at it from an outsider's perspective – what impact will your goal have on individuals and other functions within or connected to the organisation?

Decide how consultative you need to be in order to gain maximum benefits.

- Do you need to consult with anyone before rolling out the vision to others?
- Who would this be with?
- How will it be conducted?

This doesn't mean that every stage has to be negotiated but it does mean that goals should be consistent with expectations and address concerns.

## (P) riorities

It will be important for you and others actioning the strategy to be able to easily identify the priorities in order to succeed. Take into consideration the complexity of the task and make sure you prioritise critical 'milestones', tasks and actions. You could use a graph like this:

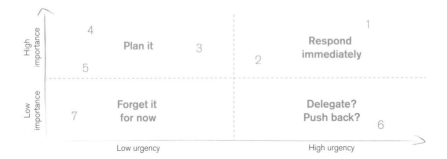

Involve others if possible, to agree the top three to five goals, and then prioritise them. In order to temper ideas you could ensure someone always plays 'devil's advocate' – challenging or testing suggestions before acceptance.

**pportunities**

In addition to the benefits and opportunities of the overall goal, consider what each person involved has to gain from the process of working towards it, including development opportunities, reward and recognition. Examine how you will delegate tasks and the potential opportunities they offer – see the tool 'How to delegate' for more advice on this subject.

Finally, consider your own gains including development, an improved profile in the organisation and increased self-esteem.

**isks**

Differentiate between the strategy's perceived and actual risks or threats. Consult with others if necessary to find ways of offsetting them. Make these preparations known to mitigate concern and strengthen support for the strategy.

Using the list of prioritised actions, identify their foremost 'issues'. Make sure you continue to do this as your plan progresses – and especially in the short to medium term; that is, the next couple of months or year.

Of potential risk to all strategies is how people manage and deal with change. Consider how complex the tasks are and how this will fit in with workloads, or otherwise affect people. How you manage change for yourself and others is critical to maintaining commitment and momentum. To this end, manage the impact of change by giving information and feedback during the process, through regular reviews of team and individual progress.

**imelines**

Consider your plan in a broader context. For example, keep an eye on what's going on in the marketplace and factor in economic and societal trends, competitor activity and new developments. You could use a model such as PEST(LE)[3] to help focus your thoughts here. Also, think about the internal position and how this may affect your strategy by considering: Where is the organisation heading? What will the situation look like in the future?

Think about aspects such as timescales, resources which might be needed (people – role modelling, money, time, your own personal qualities of perseverance, etc.) and financial requirements. Make this as definitive as possible – the S.M.A.R.T. technique[4] for goal setting will be useful. Make your goals specific, realistic and measurable – and explain why they're worthwhile. Celebrate achievements along the way. How will you know what these smaller achievements are? How will you get feedback to use as evidence of them?

If you follow these simple rules, your strategic goal setting process will be much more successful and your overall performance will improve.

The following pages outline three practical tools to help you to develop strategic long-term goals:

- Strategic Goal Setting Checklist
- Common Barriers to Success and Remedy Advice
- V-SPORT Self-Analysis.

# ● STRATEGIC GOAL SETTING CHECKLIST

To help you ensure you're covering all the important aspects of developing strategic goals, you could use this checklist (print it out if it's easier). It conforms with the 'V-SPORT' model outlined earlier.

Tick off sections as you complete them.

| | Strategic Goal Setting Checklist | |
|---|---|---|
| **V** | 1. Write your vision down, ensuring that it is easy to understand and clear in providing a focus. | |
| | 2. Test the vision with key stakeholders in order to ensure that you are moving in a mutually agreed direction. | |
| | 3. Consider, and note down, some of the broader benefits for the organisation, external customers, your team and yourself. | |
| | 4. Formulate some clear long-term goals which fit in with your vision. These should form the basis of your strategy. | |
| **S** | 5. Reflect on who your internal and external customers are and note them down. | |
| | 6. Be clear who your key stakeholders in the project are and how you are going to involve them in the process. | |
| | 7. Decide on the level of consultation you need with stakeholders, customers and your team. | |
| | 8. Think about who the end users are, or those who will be affected by the overall outcome, and ensure this is factored into your plan. | |
| **P** | 9. Write down the goals you're trying to achieve and prioritise them in order of importance for overall success. | |
| | 10. Consider the current situation and future changes to try to anticipate whether priorities may need to change over time. | |
| | 11. Prioritise actions in terms of importance and urgency. | |
| | 12. Identify the support you'll require and from whom to complete tasks, especially those of high priority. | |
| **O** | 13. Identify the overall benefits of the strategy and prioritise them. | |
| | 14. Consider the benefits and opportunities for people working to deliver the strategy, to motivate and recognise or reward them. | |
| | 15. Outline the benefits to customers and stakeholders. | |
| | 16. Put together a 'benefits business case' outlining the main positives in order to sell the vision to others. | |
| **R** | 17. Conduct an analysis of the risks and threats that exist or could potentially arise to threaten success. | |
| | 18. Categorise these risks and threats into high, medium and low categories. | |
| | 19. Identify the major issues you foresee over the short, medium and long-term and categorise them in terms of importance and urgency. | |
| | 20. Attend to those issues which are 'most important and urgent' first, then those which are 'important not urgent' and then the 'urgent not important' ones. | |
| **T** | 21. Think about how your vision and strategy fits in with broader organisational goals. | |
| | 22. Look at the factors that could affect your strategy. You could use a model such as PEST(LE) to help focus your thoughts here. | |
| | 23. Consider changes to the internal position and how this may affect your strategy: 'where is the organisation heading in the future?' | |
| | 24. Factor in current competitor/comparator data or activity and try to forecast future changes that may affect success. | |

# ● COMMON BARRIERS TO SUCCESS & REMEDY ADVICE

In developing strategic long-term goals, people experience a number of common barriers. You may even be facing one or two of these right now! Some are outlined below with a little guidance for overcoming them.

| Barrier | Remedy Advice |
| --- | --- |
| The goal is complex and you don't know how you will be able to achieve it in practice | ● Manage expectations by giving people sufficient time to meet the goal or improve performance. <br><br> ● Provide time for practice or learning what is expected and required for success. <br><br> ● Make the 'milestones' as specific as possible so you can keep on top of them. <br><br> ● Consider the 'pinch points' you might be facing, from future events – situations that you know are likely to, or will, arise. |
| You are devoid of ideas on how to develop the initial concept | ● Take a wide-ranging look around at what's going on both inside and outside the organisation which might affect it, using an 'environmental scan' or a SWOT analysis. <br><br> ● Establish statements of mission, vision and priority actions/issues. <br><br> ● You may want to refer to the 'How to think about problems laterally' tool to help you develop the concept. |
| You are struggling to think of how your plan fits in with future challenges | ● Be clear what your overall objective is and how this fits in with the bigger picture. <br><br> ● Consider where the organisation or your department might be in the future, e.g. in the next 6 months, next year, next couple of years, etc. <br><br> ● Be clear what the risks are – consider doing a simple risk analysis. |
| You have an idea but are not sure who to consult with and at which stage to get it accepted | ● Consider who the key stakeholders are in the process. Is this your plan or are you implementing someone else's vision? <br><br> ● Also, think about who the end users might be or who may be affected by the outputs of the strategy or need to be involved along the way; for example, your internal or external customers. <br><br> ● You could set up a forum such as a steering committee to look at the idea or you may want to put together a business plan or proposal to 'sell' the idea or the benefits to others to gain their buy-in. |

# ● V-SPORT SELF-ANALYSIS

In order for you to consider your approach to developing strategic long-term goals use the following tool to highlight your relative strengths and aspects in need of development in all the V-SPORT dimensions.

## Step 1: Complete the self-analysis questionnaire

Complete the self-analysis questionnaire using the Red (R), Amber (A), Green (G) system. Write in the corresponding letter (R, A or G) using the key on the next page.

**Key:**

Red – This is an aspect that you struggle to achieve, or find difficult. You may put it off or try to delegate it to others to complete.

Amber – You can complete this quite easily. It may not be the most fascinating or easy stage for you but you can, and will, tend to do this.

Green – This is what you excel at and find easy. You may put more effort into this stage and find it motivating or enjoyable to complete.

| Strategic Goal Setting Self-Analysis | | R | A | G |
|---|---|---|---|---|
| **V** | 1. Creating a clear focus to aim for. | | | |
| | 2. Thinking broadly to consider the business and the market. | | | |
| | 3. Looking at the future implications of the vision for the business. | | | |
| **S** | 4. Identifying all of the key internal and external customers. | | | |
| | 5. Being clear about how to involve people in making the vision happen. | | | |
| | 6. Factoring the needs of stakeholders into your strategy. | | | |
| **P** | 7. Being clear about the actions to prioritise. | | | |
| | 8. Knowing how to prioritise in terms of urgency and importance. | | | |
| | 9. Considering changes that may affect how you prioritise at the outset. | | | |
| **O** | 10. Highlighting the main benefits that may happen as a result. | | | |
| | 11. Thinking about opportunities for everyone involved in the process. | | | |
| | 12. Identifying short-term wins as well as longer-term gains. | | | |
| **R** | 13. Identifying all of the risks and threats which might de-rail the process. | | | |
| | 14. Considering contingency plans to overcome the challenges. | | | |
| | 15. Prioritising the issues in terms of importance and urgency. | | | |
| **T** | 16. Thinking broadly about the current situation and context. | | | |
| | 17. Forecasting the future to pre-empt changes and allow for them in your plan. | | | |
| | 18. Looking at the wider marketplace to understand how your strategy fits into the bigger picture. | | | |

## Step 2: Scoring the self-analysis questionnaire

Use the following 2-step process to score your results.

1. Look at each category and add the corresponding Red (R), Amber (A), Green (G) ratings to formulate your unique combination. An example has been completed for you:

Example:

| Area | Items to Add | Combination |
|------|------|------|
| V | 1-3 | R-A-G |

Your Template to Complete:

| Area | Items to Add | Combination |
|------|------|------|
| V | 1-3 | |
| S | 4-6 | |
| P | 7-9 | |
| O | 13-16 | |
| R | 17-20 | |
| T | 21-24 | |

2. Now, record your strengths and aspects in need of development in the Strength/ Development summary below. Use the table to help you translate your combination into the relevant Strength/Development category:

| Combinations | | Strength/Development |
|------|------|------|
| G-G-G | G-G-A | Significant strength |
| G-G-R | G-A-A | Strength |
| A-A-A | G-A-R | Average/mixed |
| G-R-R | A-A-R | Development need |
| A-R-R | R-R-R | Significant development need |

## Strength/Development Summary

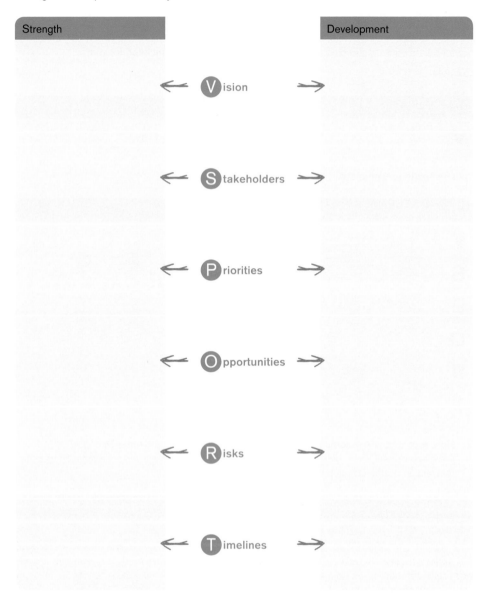

## Step 3: Consider your strengths and development needs

Now you've identified your stronger and weaker areas think about how you can capitalise on your strengths and what you might need to do to improve your weaker areas. Consider the following questions to help you focus your thoughts:

- How can you capitalise on your strongest areas?

- How can you use your areas of strength to support you in your development areas?

- What support do you need to work on your development needs?

- What barriers do you face to improving your development needs?

- How would you overcome these barriers?

- What would make the biggest overall difference to you in developing strategic goals?

## Communication

Consider how you will communicate your vision or strategy to others involved in carrying out the work or those who will be affected by the proposal. This should always be clear and concise with consideration given to recipients' requirements – how much detail people need. Also consider whether they need to know the whole process or focus on certain aspects, such as giving each employee a card with the mission statement on it or publishing portions of your plan in a regular newsletter.

## ● NEXT STEPS

Now that you have considered the factors involved in developing successful strategies and long-term goals and have some practical tools to consider, it's worth thinking about what to do next. Here are a number of suggestions (although these are by no means exhaustive):

### Develop operational plan

Write a rough plan of the resources, budget and timing that you need to make the strategy happen. This doesn't have to be precise but should be as accurate as you can forecast.

### Look for opportunities to practise

Think about the opportunities you have in your current work, or outside of your existing remit where you can support or lead on developing strategic long-term goals.

### Implement the advice

Try and implement some of the advice or practical tools outlined in this document when next developing a strategy.

### Gather feedback on existing performance

You may find it useful to consider your current strengths and development needs for creating visions and strategic planning. Benchmarking your current performance by asking for formal or informal feedback will help you understand where you need most support hereafter, and may help others around you recognise your approach and needs.

## ● FURTHER INFORMATION

If you found this tool useful then you are likely to find the following tools both insightful and relevant:

- How to think about problems laterally
- How to formulate action plans
- How to communicate your vision
- How to be innovative
- How to focus on the bigger picture
- How to make ethical decisions
- How to balance risk with potential benefits.

## ● REFERENCES

1   Read, D. & van Leeuwen, B. (1998). Predicting Hunger: The Effects of Appetite and Delay on Choice. **Organizational Behavior and Human Decision Processes,** 76(2), 189-205.

2   Loewenstein, G., O'Donoghue, T. & Rabin, M. (2003). Projection Bias In Predicting Future Utility. **Quarterly Journal of Economics,** 118(4), 1209-1248.

3   Johnson, G. & Scholes, K.R.W. (2006). **Exploring Corporate Strategy,** Prentice Hall.

4   Doran, George T. (1981), There's a S.M.A.R.T Way to Write Management Goals and Objectives, **Management Review** (AMA Forum).

# HOW TO BE INNOVATIVE

Find out where innovation and creativity come from and how they can be harnessed for yourself and encouraged in those around you.

## ● ISN'T IT INTERESTING?

What do you see in the image to the right?

### Just an apple?

To most people, this is just an apple. However, to one exceptional scientist it was the inspiration for the greatest leap forward in physics since the Ancient Greeks. Whilst the story of Newton's apple might just be anecdotal, it serves to explain that even the most subtle cues can be the source of the most creative and innovative ideas. To explain further, the classic psychological experiment below shows how great ideas can be born from the most inauspicious starts.

### Monkey-ing around

If you've ever seen chimpanzees at a zoo, you might be aware of their tendency to behave in a cheeky manner. However, to psychologists, this unruly behaviour can be indicative of a much more complex psychological premise. And due to our evolutionary closeness to chimpanzees, this makes it all the more relevant to our understanding of the human mind.

A 2010 study[1] into chimpanzees kept in a zoo in Sweden focused on the questionable actions of Sandino, a Bonobo chimp. Sandino was fond of throwing rocks and other objects at the visitors to the zoo who disturbed his peaceful existence. In an effort to stop this, the zoo keepers removed any throwable objects during visiting times. This was not enough, however, to stop Sandino, who had learnt to hide objects under hay and other materials, ready for the visitors' arrival.

It was known before this study that intelligent animals such as chimps are able to display forward planning such as this. But critically, this behaviour was self-generated and not the process of a labratory-based study, in which Sandino was being conditioned into a desired behaviour. Additionally, Sandino had not copied this behaviour from another chimp or human; it was a truly innovative behaviour. This means chimpanzees have the ability to spontaneously generate innovative ideas to achieve an aim.

## This tool can help

This classic research neatly describes how creativity and innovation can be prompted by almost anything. This tool is about **how to be innovative** and provides you with insight into where innovation and creativity come from and how they can be harnessed for yourself and encouraged in those around you.

# ● WHY FOCUS ON INNOVATION?

Everyone is capable of innovation and all jobs require it. Any job that does not require the ability to produce a unique output or solution is probably already being done by a machine or a computer. While it comes more easily to some than others – depending on personality, aptitude, motivation and training – we all have brains that are evolved for creative problem solving and innovation.

So why don't we get the chance – or indeed give ourselves the chance? A lot of the answer lies in the stereotypes we have of ourselves, of our employees or of specific job roles. If we see ourselves as operating primarily in the 'task' domain (i.e. we tend to focus on the importance of completing tasks quickly and effectively), we might simply not give ourselves time to step over into the 'thought' domain and flex our more innovative muscles.

## Definitions

Innovation means the process of coming up with new ideas, processes, solutions or products. It means tackling a challenge in a way that has not been tried before. It does not necessarily mean invention. You can innovate by applying an existing solution in a novel way or by combining solutions to tackle a new problem. So, innovation means doing something different, but it doesn't have to mean starting from scratch. Indeed, Benjamin Franklin suggested that a definition of insanity was 'doing the same thing over and over again and expecting different results'! This is why everyday innovation is important. More than half the battle is to ask the question: 'could we be doing this differently?'

## Climate and barriers

The climate that we work in is a key determinant of how much of our capacity to innovate we bring to work with us. Do we work – or encourage others to work – in a 'yes...but' environment where analysis overrides original thinking? Do we work – or encourage others to work – in an environment where controls and metrics mean that there is little opportunity and little encouragement to try out new things? Does our climate reward systemisation more than speculation? An unsupportive business environment will make it all the more likely that we will save our moments of innovation – be they a daily or a yearly event – for the weekend.

## Key questions to foster innovation

A simple way to encourage innovation – your own or others – is to ask the right questions. In our own work we have developed five key questioning areas which encourage open-ended thinking about a situation or challenge. These always ensure multiple perspectives are considered in framing a solution or a new idea.

These questioning areas are outlined in the model on the next page.

# ● FIVE KEY QUESTIONING AREAS

The following five questioning areas can be used to encourage innovation and open-ended thinking.[2] Each of these areas is discussed in more detail on the next page.

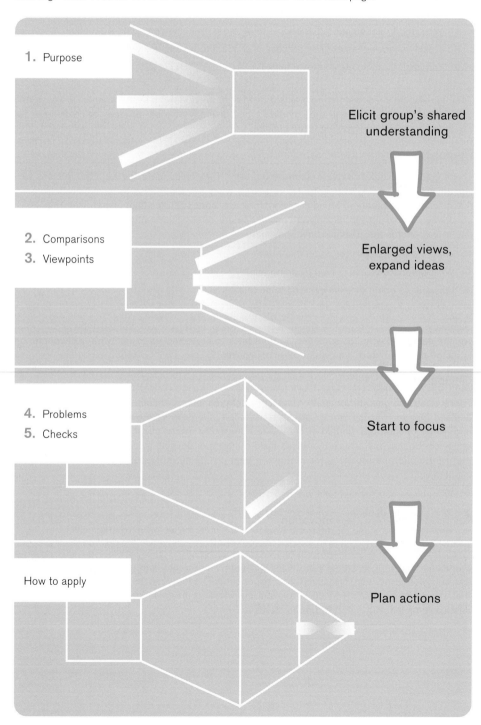

1. Purpose

Elicit group's shared understanding

2. Comparisons
3. Viewpoints

Enlarged views, expand ideas

4. Problems
5. Checks

Start to focus

How to apply

Plan actions

## ● WHEN TO USE THE KEY QUESTIONS

The key questions can be used when:

- You or your team are feeling 'stuck' about finding a solution or new idea
- You need to encourage other people to be more open minded about a situation
- 'Reality checking' an existing process or product to test its utility
- You need to stimulate your own thinking.

They can also be used to structure brainstorming or problem-solving sessions which are designed to open up people's minds to the complexity and diversity of a set of ideas or challenges, for example when dealing with significant change.

## Purpose:

These questions seek to explore issues about 'why'. They help clarify and align the reasons why something is happening or help to define exactly what it is that needs to be achieved. Purpose questions tend to be about broad direction; they are more strategic than operational. They are a good way of opening up thinking to consider future possibilities rather than staying rooted in day-to-day operations. Examples might include:

- What are the reasons for doing this?
- What purposes will be served by doing this?
- Why are we doing this/do we need to do this?
- Why are we doing this now?

**Summary:** Your answers to the above questions will provide you with the initial picture of what you are doing and why. You should try to refer back to these replies so that what you do later on in the process still fits in with your overall objectives.

## Comparisons:

These questions are designed to force consideration of experience and prior learning; they demand that you put the current issue or challenge alongside your own (or the organisation's) knowledge of what has worked or not worked previously. These questions are more than just a reality check, they make sure that ideas build rather than develop in isolation. They also ensure that all the relevant information is brought to bear on the current issue or challenge. Examples might include:

- What happened the last time we tried this?
- Who else has done this – what did they learn?
- How is this the same (or different) from similar situations we have experienced?
- What factors do we want to change to reach a different/better outcome?

**Summary:** Gathering responses to these questions ensures that you have looked into the past and considered the learning gained from experience. These questions are useful to make sure that you are not constantly trying to reinvent the wheel. It may also be that something from the past could be innovative in the current situation.

## Viewpoints:

These questions stimulate consideration of multiple viewpoints and test your thinking about the perceptions and involvement of stakeholders. They are not meant to be about how to present something to different audiences, but a genuine 'eye opener' in terms of how other groups might see things. Viewpoint questions force you to take a different stance and thus open up possibilities. Examples might include:

- How would this issue/opportunity look to our employees/shareholders/families/ communities/neighbours/competitors/customers?
- How would an expert frame this issue; what different questions would they ask?
- How would an enemy see this issue; how would an ally see it?

**Summary:** These questions are all about expanding your thinking to see things from as many angles as possible. It is especially important at this stage to think about who the stakeholders and customers are and how they would view the situation. This will help later on in the process when trying to gain buy-in to your idea(s).

## Problems:

As well as helping to anticipate pitfalls or barriers to success, these questions are about visualising the future and testing your thinking by asking 'what if?' It is important that they are not used in a 'yes...but' way; they should be used to test ideas rather than to stifle them. So, as well as testing the robustness of your ideas or solutions, they help to make sure that you have considered a range of eventualities. Examples might include:

- What could stop this from working? What could go wrong?
- What if (X) changed, how would that affect things?
- How will we overcome any obstacles we anticipate?

**Summary:** Your replies should help formulate potential ideas and solutions. Try to remain as open as possible to give full consideration to the ideas being discussed.

## Checks:

These questions are the only truly operational questions on the list; however, they are not meant to be about monitoring, but about visualising a course of events to see how success will be achieved.

Fundamentally they are about creating a clear picture of success and they also set up the possibility of continuous innovation, making you consider progress stages and build in responsiveness and realignment. Examples might include:

- How will we know if we are succeeding; what will tell us that things are better?
- What will success look like; what are our success criteria?
- What will be the signs that we should stop and try something else?

**Summary:** These questions help you to future plan and to map out what success looks like. Give this section enough time to ensure that the concept you have considered meets your original purpose and you have a strategy to make it a success.

Consider the following example of a toy company trying to come up with a new toy for Christmas:

| Key Questions | Example Replies |
|---|---|
| **Purpose questions**<br>● What are the reasons for doing this?<br>● What purposes will be served by doing this?<br>● Why are we doing this/do we need to do this?<br>● Why are we doing this now? | We are trying to come up with a new toy for Christmas that is going to wow the kids and be a best seller.<br><br>We need the sales as this is the busiest time of the year and we will all get bonuses if this is a success. |
| **Comparisons questions**<br>● What happened the last time we tried this?<br>● Who else has done this – what did they learn?<br>● How is this the same (or different) from similar situations we have experienced?<br>● What factors or variables do we want to change to reach a different/better outcome? | Last year we only got to number 25 with our interactive board game and number 12 with the latest type of rollerblade.<br><br>We need to consider the current trends towards health and exercise as well as computers. Or do we need to go back to a more simple toy?<br><br>We need to learn from our competitors e.g. last year's top toys – the smart cycle, cartoon character masks and toy electric guitar. |
| **Viewpoints questions**<br>● How would this (issue/opportunity) look to our employees/shareholders/families/communities/neighbours/competitors/customers?<br>● How would a technical expert/non expert frame this issue; what different questions would they ask?<br>● How would an enemy see this issue; how would an ally see it? | We need to conduct focus groups with kids, parents, teachers and suppliers.<br><br>We need to think about what is going to be big for girls and boys, and what age we are aiming for, and ask about these different groups.<br><br>We need to talk to our suppliers to find out about costs for us and for the market. |
| **Problems questions**<br>● What could stop this from working? What could go wrong?<br>● What if (X) changed, how would that affect things?<br>● How will we overcome any obstacles we anticipate? | We could miss important market information, so we need to be thorough. We need to talk to a wide cross section of people.<br><br>We need to plan for changes in trends or recessions/big market/world events.<br><br>We need to be very clear on health and safety of our toy. |
| **Checks questions**<br>● How will we know if we are succeeding; what will tell us that things are better?<br>● What will success look like; what are our success criteria?<br>● What will be the signs that we should stop and try something else? | We need to know what sales we are aiming for in order to make a profit and be in the top ten.<br><br>There will be milestones that we have to be hitting in the run up to Christmas and we have to have a set launch date to maximise sales.<br><br>Our marketing needs to be as focused as possible on the target market. |

# ● MAKING INNOVATION HAPPEN

Now that you have used the questioning techniques to encourage innovation, here are some further tips to help you make innovation happen.

## Give yourself time for thought leadership

The single, clearest measure of our conscious or unconscious work priorities is how we use our time. Think of an average day, week or month and identify where your time goes. It will be unsurprising if you find that the great majority of your time goes on operational 'task' matters and that relatively little goes on thought leadership and innovation. No matter which technique for brainstorming, reframing issues, asking yourself key questions or creating a shift in your approach that you adopt, it will not thrive if you don't make time. This means recognising that innovation has a sufficiently high priority for you to devote significant time to it.

## Know yourself, know your team

Individuals vary widely in terms of strengths and risks relating to their capacity to innovate. You need to recognise these, both in yourself and in your team/colleagues. Your signature strengths – and those of your team – in relation to innovation may already be apparent to you. If you think this needs more consideration then look at some of the other diagnostics in the iLEAD™ stable; for example, Big 5 Personality Theory in 'How to identify personal learning styles' (in the People Leadership book).

## Practise innovation

Play 'just suppose' – imagine a situation where a standard assumption no longer holds true. For example, suppose that Britain had the same climate as Egypt – what would this mean; what possibilities would arise? Suppose that a law was passed cutting the working week to 20 hours – how would you do business? Suppose that your strongest product didn't exist – how would you fill the gap? Take any aspect of your business or working life that you take for granted and then throw away the assumptions.

## Reinvent the wheel

Take one of your tried and tested products or processes and work out what it would take to replace it with something better – you can bet your competition is doing just this!

## Check your personal, team and business 'innovation climate'

Ask yourself the following questions:

A. What supports or stifles innovation around here?

B. When do I have and share good ideas – do we have forums where this happens?

C. When do I feel insecure about trying something new; how can I create the conditions in which my ingenuity thrives?

D. How often does the team get together to speculate rather than to coordinate?

Above all encourage and develop skilled managers and leaders who create the conditions in which people feel free to innovate and, as important, who recognise and remove the barriers to divergent thinking. As one senior business leader told me: 'We spend a fortune recruiting the brightest, most creative and most enterprising people and then spend the next five years accidentally beating it out of them, so all their flair goes into their hobbies, their homes, their flower beds!'

## Managing risk aversion

Our brains have developed over time to make quick decisions based on limited data. The same evolutionary process has equipped us to be more vigilant of risk and threat than we are open to opportunity. Put these together and it is all too easy to arrive at a default position based on caution rather than innovation; a position that drives 'yes...but' thinking with the risk of closing down possibilities too early, rather than exploring and expanding on what might be.

What else can we do to avoid defaulting to the fastest option, the habitual option or the most risk free option?

- Challenge the tendency to make quick decisions based on tried and tested methods and categorisations.
- Seek and be open minded to fresh data/stimulus to help you think differently about issues you are presented with. Take a mental pause whenever you hear yourself saying 'yes...but'.
- Actively engage with the process of seeking new insights and challenging your existing thoughts as this will not happen by chance.

Innovation has to be nurtured; the weeds of inertia take over the garden all too easily!

## ● FURTHER INFORMATION

If you found this tool useful then you are likely to find the following tools both insightful and relevant:

- How to think about problems laterally
- How to improve processes
- How to get the most out of yourself
- How to reframe problems.

## ● REFERENCES

1 Osvath, M., & Karvonen, E. (2012). Spontaneous Innovation for Future Deception in a Male Chimpanzee. PloS one, 7(5).

2 Pearn, M., Roderick, C. & Mulrooney, C. (1995). **Learning Organizations in Practice**. Maidenhead: McGraw Hill.

# HOW TO THINK ABOUT PROBLEMS LATERALLY

Understand different thinking styles and preferences. Increase your awareness of personal styles and preferences to help you to see situations from different perspectives to your normal approach.

## ● ISN'T IT INTERESTING?

A boy was walking down the road, and came to a place where the road divided in two; each road went in a different direction. There was a girl standing at the fork in the road. The boy knew that one road led to Lieville, a town where everyone always lied, and the other led to Trueville, a town where everyone always told the truth. He also knew that the girl came from one of those towns, but he didn't know which one.

What should the boy ask the girl to find out the way to Trueville?

### Are you in or outside the box?

In 1967, Edward DeBono[1] coined the concept of 'lateral thinking' – a way of understanding concepts and rules but not being restrained by them. Albert Einstein, for example, understood classical mechanics but was still able to think laterally about issues without being constrained by these mechanics. The goal of using lateral thinking, therefore, is to shift away from thinking in an orthodox way to being more innovative in your solutions. Innovation can help you think about issues more broadly, and in ways you may have previously overlooked.

### The truth and nothing but the truth

So let's revisit the lateral thinking problem that we gave you at the beginning of the page. With the above problem you need to ask the question, 'Which way is your town?', because the girl was from Lieville, she would point to Trueville because she has to lie; if she was from Trueville, she'll point to Trueville because she has to tell the truth. So whatever road the girl points to will be the road to Trueville. Did you get it? Well, even if you didn't, lateral thinking can be learnt and trained.

### This tool can help

The important factor here is that we all see things differently and at work we need to capitalise on these differences fully to be most effective. This tool is about **how to think about problems laterally** and will help you to understand different thinking styles and preferences. Increasing your awareness of personal styles and preferences can help you to see situations from different perspectives to your normal approach.

## ● THINKING LATERALLY

We all solve problems every day or, at least, find ways round them. Mostly, we deal with things well enough, but how often have you felt there must be another way – just what or how, exactly? This is where lateral thinking comes in and it's a useful skill because, if you always think about things in the same way you could be missing the point, and much else besides. Lateral thinking is all about considering things from different perspectives and in less habitual ways. It can eliminate potential blind spots, produce alternative solutions, identify otherwise hidden opportunities and improve existing processes and methodologies.

Recognising that we all think differently from one another is the first step towards lateral thinking. There are a range of different problems and some insights about different personal preferences[2] that will help you to reflect on your own ability to think laterally.

## ● LATERAL THINKING PROBLEMS

Here are a few briefly described scenes to help you recognise your own thinking habits and start you thinking 'outside the box'. Consider the examples below[3] and see whether you can think of the solutions. The answers are given at the end of this tool – but don't peek, just work through the exercise – it'll be worth it! Write your solutions in the boxes below the examples.

### Example one

Acting on an anonymous phone call, police raid a house to arrest a suspected murderer. They don't know what he looks like, but they know his name is John and that he's inside the house. They burst in on a carpenter, a lorry driver, a mechanic and a fireman, all playing poker. Without hesitation or communication of any kind, they immediately arrest the fireman. How do they know they've got their man?

Answer

### Example two

A recluse who never left home was only visited when his food and other supplies were delivered and even then, no one went inside. One stormy, winter's night when a gale was blowing, he had what the locals later decided must have been a nervous breakdown, because he went upstairs, turned off all the lights and went to bed. Next morning, he had caused the deaths of several hundred people. How?

Answer

## Example three

Five pieces of coal, a carrot and a scarf are lying on a hill near a remote house. Nobody put them on the ground but there is a reasonable explanation for why they're there. What is it?

Answer

## Example four

A man was driving alone when he spun off the road at high speed. His car crashed through a fence and bounced down a steep ravine, before plunging into a fast flowing river. As it slowly settled in the river, the man realised his arm was broken and he couldn't release his seat belt to escape. He was trapped and the car sank. Rescuers arrived two hours later to find him still in the river and alive. How?

Answer

Now check your answers against the examples answer sheet towards the end of this tool.

**Next, think about how you came up with a solution (whether it was right or wrong):**

- What was going on in your thinking?
- How did you get to the solution?
- What errors did you make; for example, could you think of only one, familiar use for something?
- Did you make assumptions?
- Were you being too literal?
- Were you attending to the right information?

## Some things to think about…

### Example one

The first example challenges our preconceptions. We may assume that everyone in the room is male because we have a preconception that carpenters, lorry drivers and mechanics are typically men. We may also have a preconception that poker is typically played by men and not women.

**Tip:** When thinking laterally, try to challenge your own preconceptions. Keeping an open mind helps you recognise different solutions.

### Example two

We assume someone's home is a house or flat but people can live in all kinds of places. Think of where it's essential a light is kept on all the time and failure to do so would endanger lives.

**Tip:** When thinking laterally, focus on the facts and how they could be construed in different ways.

### Example three

For this example, think how things can be used for other than their usual purpose.

**Tip:** When thinking laterally, try to think of as many different uses for things as possible.

### Example four

This is about semantics. When we read about a fast flowing river and the car sinking, we assume the river's deep. The words 'high speed' and 'crashed' make us think this is a very dangerous situation.

**Tip:** When thinking laterally, challenge what at first seems obvious.

## ● THINKING STYLES

## Challenging vs. accepting

Of course, we all make assumptions all the time – things would get very tedious if we didn't assume, say, that the kettle will turn itself off, as usual. However, we also make assumptions because we often have to make quick decisions without much information, so we make a 'best fit' from the available facts – and our own previous experience.

In other words, rather than relying on the facts alone, our brains reduce processing time by referring to previous, similar situations or other related information. This is how we decide to react in certain situations, too, but it's also how we reinforce prejudice and bias – how we train ourselves to think in the same way about things all the time. Challenging our assumption that carpenters, lorry drivers and mechanics are always men, for example, makes for more objective decision making.

## Logical vs. intuitive thinking

Lateral thinking can involve logic, intuition and imagination. Had you come across pieces of coal, a carrot and scarf lying on the ground, as in example three above, your intuition might suggest it was all that was left of a snowman, and logic would explain why the snowman himself was no longer evident, having melted!

## Creative vs. literal thinking

Thinking too literally can inhibit lateral thinking because it prevents you thinking beyond the obvious. Many of us assume (there it is, again!) that we're not creative, but you'll surprise yourself if you let your imagination off the hook for a few minutes with this short exercise:

## For two minutes, think of all the things you could do with a cardboard tube!:

Here's a couple: you could cut it up and use it to support small plants or balance it on two blocks to use as a hurdle. Try to come up with workable ideas (for example, it wouldn't be much use as a fire poker, would it?)

## Experiential thinking

When thinking laterally, put yourself in the situation you're considering. Visualise yourself actually there, and visualise what you, and whoever else might be there, are doing. Try to involve as many of your senses as possible. What are you thinking, feeling, seeing, hearing, tasting and even smelling? You'll be surprised by how much more information or inspiration this yields.

## Big picture vs. detailed thinking

Sometimes, if we concentrate on detail, we 'can't see the wood for the trees'. In other words, while detail is important, we need to consider it in context to make our thinking practical and generate other, appropriate ideas. In example four on page 28, details of a car which 'crashed' and 'sank to the bottom' suggest tragedy. In fact, the driver – a bit surprised, perhaps, and no doubt a little cold and damp – was safe, sitting in his car on a shallow river's bed!

## Pictorial thinking

In the famous stories, Sherlock Holmes was a great one for visualising and sketching scenes of crime as imagined by him, or described by someone else. Try sketching what you think you would see if you were in the situation you're contemplating, to reveal perspectives you might otherwise miss.

# ● PREFERENCES

Use the table below to identify your preferred, or usual way of thinking and help you consider others. Note down your preferences, 1-3. Put a 1, 2 or 3 against the corresponding preference:

| Preferences | 1, 2 or 3 | Preferences | 1, 2 or 3 |
| --- | --- | --- | --- |
| Bigger picture | | Detail focused | |
| Creative | | Literal | |
| Logical | | Intuitive | |
| Experiential | | Observational* | |
| Pictorial | | Aural** | |
| Challenging | | Accepting*** | |

*Observational is the opposite of experiential, so someone who takes a step back from a situation.
**Aural is someone who tends to use their hearing or listening to attend to a situation.
***Accepting is the opposite of challenging and is someone who accepts the status quo.

Now consider this scenario[4] and put your answer in the box on the following page:

## Preference scenario

Two strangers from different parts of the UK build similar apartment buildings in their home towns. By chance, they both forget an item which is important to their project. They each, once again by chance, call the same national hardware store and order the missing items. The prices they are quoted are as follows:

- One will cost them £2
- Two will cost them £2
- Twelve will cost them £4
- One hundred and forty-four will cost £6.

What was the item they needed?

| Answer |
| --- |
|  |

See the preference scenario answer sheet at the end of this tool for the answer.

Now that you know what the answer is, let's see how, using your preferences, you would answer. This also gives you a chance to see how people who think in different ways may arrive at their answer:

| If you have a strong preference for... | You are likely to... |
| --- | --- |
| Bigger picture | have considered why the strangers were buying the apartments and where their home towns might be. You would have considered the overall picture and its most significant elements. For example, which building materials would be most economical and which could be bought most cheaply in bulk? |
| Detail focused | have thought about the minutiae – precisely what was the missing item needed for constructing apartment blocks? You probably focused on important information, like numbers, costs and the sort of problems encountered in construction as well the significance of needing to visit a hardware store. |
| Creative | have thought about the kind of materials used to construct apartment buildings, using your own experience or knowledge. You may have considered what style of apartment blocks they were building to work out what the missing items might be. |
| Literal | have looked at the available information and worked through it systematically, to see if any of it indicates what the missing items were. You probably focused on the price of the individual item, the different quantities and scale of costs to solve the problem. |
| Logical | have tried to establish if there were clues or logical links in the text alone. You would probably think about the likely cost of items used for this particular purpose. |
| Intuitive | have relied on your initial 'gut feeling' or instinct about a particular aspect, such as whether the pricing was correct or whether the unit cost needed to be low because of the number of items needed, etc. |

| If you have a strong preference for... | You are likely to... |
|---|---|
| Experiential | have imagined yourself in that situation, thinking about what you would need from a hardware store at those prices. |
| Observational | have adopted a slightly removed view of the situation overall, and thought strategically – starting with the cost aspect, perhaps, to work out all the different items to which it could apply. |
| Pictorial | have imagined the situation to list everything you thought you'd need if you were building apartments yourself. You may have created a 'mind map' by making notes of these thoughts or sketching images. |
| Aural | have talked out loud about the problem – to yourself or others to see how it sounded and if this would prompt a solution. |
| Challenging | have sought the answer by questioning the information; for example, why was the cost so low, or asking which particular item would cost £4 for twelve? |
| Accepting | have taken the information at face value and relied on it alone, probably concentrating on the cost as the most helpful element from which to discover the solution. |

You can see from the table above that there are many different ways to think about generating solutions. Some thought styles will feel natural to you but you can choose different methods of processing information or approaching problems. Think about the different ways you might go about solving a problem with other people – and on your own.

The following table gives you some ideas for using different thinking styles effectively.

| Preference | Tips |
|---|---|
| Bigger picture | You like to come up with ideas and instructions, so tend to produce overall strategies and consider how they relate to wider contexts. You could use your 'big picture' thinking to help detail-focused people put their contributions into context – this might generate more ideas all round, too! You could take more time to attend to the details of a situation; for example, try working 'from the inside out' to get insights not always available from your usual 'overview'. |
| Detail focused | Because you concentrate on the details of a situation, you will want to understand exactly if and how suggestions from others would work. You can provide the details which link the different elements of a solution, or help others less able to focus on detail to consider important factors they may otherwise overlook. |
| Creative | You can think of lots of ideas and unconventional solutions (you came up with quite a few uses for a cardboard tube!) You can suggest some of your 'wackier' ideas which less creative people won't have considered, but may need to rein in ones which are not related to relevant information, are impractical or ambiguous. |

| Preference | Tips |
|---|---|
| Literal | You consider the exact meaning of information given to you and can use this focus to consider the practical impact of situations or information. You may, however, find it hard to think beyond what is immediately familiar to you and find it stressful when people ask you to do things differently. Try to think beyond immediate facts, to possibilities and potential. |
| Logical | You rely on facts and data to solve problems. You can use this approach to ensure you take all relevant information into consideration. You can be too 'matter of fact' sometimes, unwilling to recognise emotional or other factors. Try to be more aware of your instinct and other senses. |
| Intuitive | You go with your first impressions and pay a lot of attention to what your senses are telling you, even when you may not be able to support this with logic or facts. You can also use your intuition to pick up more than available facts alone provide. Try to ensure your feelings don't overrule facts or subvert your judgement. |
| Experiential | You try to imagine or visualise yourself in a situation to find solutions. You can use this technique to 'live' different aspects of a situation and then consider it as a whole. You may need to take a step back and time to reflect on the problem, to weigh up and clarify your thoughts. |
| Observational | You could use this approach to coax people away from detail to find different perspectives or long-term solutions. Sometimes, you might benefit from immersing yourself more in detail to experience the immediate reality or impact of a situation on others. |
| Pictorial | You use imagery or visualisation to solve problems. This enables you to assimilate facts and other information more easily. You could turn ideas, concepts, plans and diagrams into graphic visual aids so others can better understand otherwise complex ideas. Alternatively, try talking things through with someone else or listening to yourself, just to hear how your ideas sound when described, without visual demonstration. |
| Aural | You would talk about problems or situations with others or on your own (self-talk). Hearing the information helps you recognise its important aspects and prompts solutions. Try, also, to use your other senses, especially vision, to observe more and note how much information you really 'see' when you pay attention! |
| Challenging | You challenge and question to establish missing or inconsistent information. You can, therefore, help others to question information provided. Sometimes, however, people may think you're being obstinate or confrontational, so practise using your instinct to judge when to accept what you're told, or other people's views. |
| Accepting | You accept information at face value. You can help others focus on available information rather than disputing or elaborating on it. You should, however, recognise that you are entitled to challenge something it you feel it appropriate, and do so. |

## ● HINTS AND TIPS

The following hints and tips will help you with your lateral thinking.

## Data focus

Think about what you can learn from the information you have. Ask yourself the following questions:

- What are the gaps in your knowledge?
- What is your intuition about the situation?
- What 'gut reactions' and emotions do you have?
- What would you say if you were thinking cautiously and defensively about this situation?
- Why might things not work out?
- What can you put in place to avoid this happening?
- What would the optimistic view of this situation be?
- If you were to think creatively about this issue, what solutions would you suggest?

## Provocation

Suggest a deliberately provocative solution to a problem, one that seems 'silly' or not politically correct, perhaps. Doing this often alters our own perspective and can initiate ideas which can then be refined into realistic and successful solutions. (Don't forget, you're doing this for a constructive reason, not just to stir things up!)

## Challenge

Remember to challenge the way things are done. Never do something just because it's always been done a particular way.

## Modelling

Compare whatever problem you're mulling over now, to something entirely different – just to get the creative juices flowing. So, imagine it's a bottle of coke! Say, for example, your boss wants you to come up with an idea for a new product.

First you might think about packaging – how it looks to the outside world. Then, you might think about branding – what it 'means'. You might actually think about the stuff inside – the product. Then, what about the bubbles – this product can move, explode, even! Finally, think about production costs – how much do you need for each stage of the process?

## Challenge your assumptions

Think about the decision you've made and what evidence you have that it's the right one. Check the supporting evidence for any assumptions you have made and, if there isn't any, think of alternatives.

## Don't take things literally

If you take things too literally you might miss alternatives. Try considering more imaginative ideas and the opportunities these might create. Don't dismiss these as unrealistic or unworkable, without giving them a chance.

## Be creative

As we said earlier, think of different uses for things – not just the obvious and familiar, and do use some of the techniques described in this tool.

## Use your senses

Many of us don't pay enough attention to our full range of senses. Try not to rely just on sight, thought or intuition, but 'absorb' as much information as you can using whichever senses you usually ignore; listen more closely, pay attention to smaller details to fully appreciate how you and others feel in any situation.

## Ask other people how they do it

Ask some people you know to have a go at the examples in this tool. If they think of the right answer, ask them how they did so and use this learning to approach a similar situation differently, next time.

## How does this apply to work?

You can apply lateral thinking to many aspects of your work from problem solving to creativity. The following is a list of benefits or insights made possible by making the effort to think just a little differently from the way you usually do:

- Being innovative
- Adapting – thinking of new/better processes and ways of doing things
- Problem solving
- Decision making – thinking of different possibilities
- Spotting opportunities
- Forming strategies
- Spotting potential challenges
- Research opportunities
- Employees – have different strengths and want to be treated differently.

## ● EXAMPLE ANSWER SHEET

The answers to Lateral Thinking problems are:

## Example one

The fireman is the only man in the room, everyone else is a woman.

## Example two

He was a lighthouse keeper!

(Just because you might be interested, the first electric light in the form of carbon arc lamps was used in at Dungeness, England, in 1862).

In the beginning of the 20th century, Swedish inventor Gustav Dahlén invented the AGA Lighthouse, putting lighthouse keepers out of a job. However, many continued for years because they provided a rescue service, too. Later still, improvements in maritime navigation and safety, including GPS, led to the phasing out of nonautomated lighthouses and most of the last keepers left during the 1990s – there are still a few around, though.

## Example three

Children made a snowman with them, but, of course, he melted away with the rest of the winter's snow.

## Example four

The river water was only deep enough to reach the driver's chest.

### Preference scenario answer sheet

The items needed were door numbers. Each digit costs £2.

So the cost breakdown for the four numbers required is as follows:

- There is 1 digit in 1 and this therefore costs £2
- There is 1 digit in 2 and this therefore costs £2
- There are 2 digits in 12 and this therefore costs £4
- There are 3 digits in 144 and this therefore costs £6.

## ● FURTHER INFORMATION

If you found this tool useful then you are likely to find the following tools both insightful and relevant:

- How to be innovative
- How to reframe problems
- How to focus on the bigger picture
- How to get the most out of yourself.

## ● REFERENCES

1  De Bono, E (1970). **Lateral Thinking.** Penguin Books.

2  Myers, I. & Myers, P. (1995). **Gifts Differing: Understanding Personality Type.** Mountain View, CA: Davies-Black Publishing.

3  http://www.folj.com/lateral/fanciful.htm

4  Adapted from http://www.folj.com/lateral/fanciful.htm

# HOW TO REFRAME PROBLEMS

Understand how you can think about and successfully solve issues using a fresh perspective.

## ● ISN'T IT INTERESTING?

What do you see in this picture?

### The human brain…

Is a complex and largely mysterious organ. Our brains are able to process the outside world and help us to interact with it. Amazingly, our brain allows us to take different perspectives and see things from many alternative angles. Our brains are adaptable and fill in information gaps so we function without being overwhelmed with the amount of information in the world. So when you look at the picture here, depending on the perspective your brain chooses to take, you will see a different figure.

### So, how does this work?

In this picture you may see a young woman or an old lady. Can you see both of them? If you see the young woman and cannot see the old lady, then look at the side of the young woman's face and chin as this is the old lady's nose. The young woman's ear is the old lady's eye. Can you now see both?

This optical illusion is called an ambiguous cognitive illusion[1] and demonstrates how our brains can take the same piece of information and see different meanings. This means that what we see and do is dependent on our experience and perspective. We can use our innate ability to see different perspectives to reframe challenges. In this picture whilst our brains initially see one image, by attending to different elements we're able to change what we see. So, on viewing the picture for a second time we can see an alternative image using the same information, which is both interesting and potentially useful for us.

### This tool can help

At times, it can be difficult to understand how we can change our perspective or approach to think about issues in a different way. This tool is about how to reframe problems and will help you to understand how we can think about and successfully solve issues using a fresh perspective.

# ● WHY REFRAME PROBLEMS?

We all know how we like to do things – ways that work best for us. Whether it's preparing for a presentation, managing a team or just the way we begin our day. Once we discover methods that achieve an acceptable result, we decide they're successful and stick to them – they become habits of thinking and doing. This is mostly fine, except on those occasions when things don't work out so well. Then, we tend to think it's the task or issue in hand that's the problem rather than the way we're dealing with it. And there will always be things that stump us at work and elsewhere, which is what the ability to 'reframe problems' is all about.

## Innovative or creative?

Although these words are often used interchangeably, there's a subtle difference. People think only artistic people are 'creative' but creativity is just an ability to think originally and imaginatively about anything, plus the routine skills necessary for realisation. 'Innovation' is a new process or way of doing things. The What If![2] creative agency have defined 'creativity' as a behaviour and 'innovation' as a process. It's easy to understand why we get confused! Think of 'innovation' as the process of putting new, imaginative ('creative') ideas into practice.

## Pre-cursors to thinking creatively about problems at work

### How do our brains work?

Well, even a summary of all the research into this subject would make your head spin. However, for the purpose of understanding how to reframe problems, here are some explanatory insights:

- Our brains have evolved over time to make quick decisions based on limited information.
- Often our 'gut reactions' are informed by years of experience and other influences. We tend to categorise information to help make sense of the world around us. However, sometimes our categorisations are over simplified and not sufficient for considering new interpretations and responses, so we tend to revert to familiar, tried and tested methods.

We weren't originally 'programmed' or inclined to review our decisions in depth by searching for and making comparisons with additional or alternative information – and there wasn't much point either, when our option was usually to fight or flee. No time to mess around – go with your gut!

But things – and we – are very different now. Habitual methods and interpretations can close off the variety of options available and stunt creativity, unless we:

- Challenge the tendency to make decisions based on tried and tested methods and categorisations.
- Actively seek and be open to new information or approaches to stimulate different ways of thinking about familiar issues.

## Learnt behaviour?

There has been much debate about whether creativity is an innate ability or can be learned. It's true that there are those who, less constrained by convention, are more adept at generating ideas, but it's often only a matter of approaching issues from a different perspective – and there are techniques for this which can be learned.

## How the creative process works

1. Insight – recognise either the challenges or the opportunities (or both) of the issue you're considering.
2. Ideas – develop ideas to realise the opportunities.
3. Impact – develop a strategy for making those ideas happen.

Steps 1 and 2 are best approached with an open and reflective thought process so it helps for you to be in the right frame of mind. The next section will describe ways to break us out of an unsuitable frame of mind so we are able to effectively reframe challenges.

# ● HOW TO STOP CURRENT THOUGHT PROCESSES

Everyday activities can put you in a narrow and un-creative state of thinking, and sometimes taking a small step away from work can, in fact, help you tackle it better. A book by C. Barez-Brown explains some easy and productive breaks that can help you 'break-out' from an unimaginative rut. Some of his helpful tips are listed below.

## State breakers[3]

| What is it? | How does it work? |
|---|---|
| Get physical – go for a walk, make a cup of tea | ● Changing your physical surroundings stimulates you visually and physically.<br>● By focusing on something else you can free your mind from obstructing thoughts. |
| Count your blessings exercise | ● Without censoring your thoughts just note down anything and everything you can think of that's working well in your life, or that you appreciate.<br>● Read the list back and notice if and how your mood changes. |
| Use a 'park board' | ● On an individual or group basis capture, on a flip chart or note pad, all of the nagging doubts/creative 'blockers' you're thinking about that are dominating your thoughts and obstructing new ones.<br>● Seal the list in an envelope, psychologically 'park' them and block their recurrence until you give yourself permission to re-open the envelope later. |
| Reframe the situation | ● Write down all your feelings and concerns about the issue and your reasons for them.<br>● Reconsider what you've written, later, from a more positive – or even an amusing – perspective. |
| Ask yourself some weighty questions | In order to connect with your personal 'motivators' ask yourself the following:<br>● What in life do you want to achieve?<br>● What do you want to be remembered for?<br>● What impact would you like to have on the world?<br>● What are your passions?<br>● What would you like to learn? |

# ● BEGIN TO REFRAME PROBLEMS

The first step when reframing any problem is to recognise where the difficulty or opportunity is. Once you have identified the issue take some time to understand the nature of the problem or opportunity.

## Insight

Once you've managed to put your usual thoughts about the issue on hold, try one of the following ways to generate other ideas or insights:

## Off the top of your head

- Find someone uninvolved to listen to your description of the issue.
- Talk to them freely for as long as you can, describing the situation as fully as you can. Aim for at least 5 minutes.
- While talking, write down anything that seems interesting, strange or unusual about what you're describing.
- Your friend then responds in a similarly open way, telling you what they've heard and any ideas that occur to them.
- You then describe your feelings about their observations for 2 minutes.
- Write down any insights you've gained from the process.

## Use Post-its

- Use post-it notes to write down all your ideas about the issue.
- Then, draw a circle on a flip chart and stick the post-its you want to keep inside it.
- Look at the circle of ideas and ask yourself why you think they're plausible. Then, list anything that might prevent them succeeding.

## Ask why and how?

- For example: 'How can I secure the organisation's future?'

### Ask why?

- To ensure we keep our competitive edge.
- To bring fresh ideas from outside our organisation.

### Then ask how?

- Revisit our marketing techniques to ensure they reach as wide a talent pool as possible.
- By reviewing and implementing current recruitment best practice.

Keep asking why and how, recording your answers as you go until you run out of them.

## Ideas

There's a difference between thoughts and ideas. A thought is **'I'm bored'**, and the resulting idea: **'I'll call a friend to meet up with'**. To turn a thought into an idea and then action, ask:

- How will that work?
- What do I need to do to turn that into action?
- What might that look like if I could see it?

## Stimuli

Do something to break your train of thought and familiar method of categorisation, as we described earlier, to let in a different perspective:

- Watch a film related to the issue.
- Find an analogy or similar object, process or job.
- Play a game.
- Use magazine cuttings to represent the issue visually. Collect random items to use when trying to generate new ideas with a group. For example: 'How is the problem with our customer helpline like or unlike a bottle of Coca-Cola?' It's fun – which is one of the best ways to get people thinking creatively.

## Borrow ideas

Borrow ideas from other contexts instead of trying to 're-invent the wheel'. For example, you might want to make people more aware of health and safety issues by researching and discussing famous, major disasters which have resulted from minor causes or lapses in personal and collective responsibility. Ask people to consider the possible implications of similar behaviour in your own place of work.

## See it from another angle

Re-define the issue with one of the following techniques:

**Brain drop**

- Keep a notepad or create a wall chart for ideas about a particular issue as they come up, rather than trying to force them at a particular a time.
- Use materials that help you feel creative – coloured pens, crayons, etc.
- Try not to censor your thoughts; write down everything and then revisit it to see what could be developed.

**How might a child see this?**

- Try to let go of your preoccupations and imagine how a young child might see the issue – this could reduce it to its basic elements and reveal a new insight or solution.

**Draw it**

- Sketch it. Imagine you're explaining the idea to a client by drawing on a flipchart – it may help explain it more clearly to yourself and highlight things you've overlooked.
- Find different words to describe the issue. We use particular buzz words and other jargon without considering what they really mean or their appropriateness in a particular context. For example, find replacements for the word 'diversity' to consider its practical implications in terms of employment law.

# ● USE A REFRAMING MATRIX

People approach problems in different ways. Think of the way someone you know might deal with yours.

Write a few words representing the problem in the centre of a grid. Use the surrounding boxes to describe the different ways you think others might interpret it – and what they'd suggest.

Use the grid to look at the issue/opportunity from the following viewpoints: Product, Planning, Potential and People.

**Product perspective:** Is there something wrong with the product?

**Planning perspective:** Are business or marketing plans faulty?

**Potential perspective:** If targets were increased, how would we achieve them?

**People perspective:** Why do people choose one product over another?

Reframing Matrix Example – New product not selling well

Product perspective:
- Untried product
- Is it technically correct?
- Is it attractive?
- It is well priced?

Planning perspective:
- Are we approaching the right markets?
- Are we using the right sales strategy?

**Problem
New product
not selling**

Potential perspective:
- How would we raise sales?

Product perspective:
- How do customers see the product?
- Are they convinced that it is reliable?
- Why are they choosing other products?

## ● NEXT STEPS

We'll end with a quick summary of some of the ideas we've given you to reframe problems for success:

- A 'problem' may be an opportunity in disguise; crack it open with one or more of the techniques we've described, under the different headings in this tool:
  - Be aware of the 'creative process': 1. Insight  2. Ideas  3. Impact
  - State breakers
  - Looking at it from different angles
  - Borrowing ideas
  - Stimuli
  - Using the reframing matrix.

By using, remembering and practising these steps you will have a formidable array of tactics ready to deploy when a reframing is necessary. Always remember to be ready to accept that a reframe may be needed and to analyse how and when to go about it for the best results.

Use mood or 'state' breakers to stop your current thought process. Find which works best for you.

## ● FURTHER INFORMATION

If you found this tool useful then you are likely to find the following tools both insightful and relevant:

- How to be innovative
- How to think about problems laterally
- How to prioritise tasks ready for action
- How to focus on the bigger picture
- How to make complex ideas simple, clear and concise
- How to cope with setbacks
- How to use optimism to achieve.

## ● REFERENCES

1   Myers, D. (2003). **Psychology in Modules,** (7th ed.) New York: Worth.

2   Allan, D., Kingdon, M., Murrin, K. & Rudkin, D (2002) Sticky Wisdom. **How to Start a Creative Revolution at Work.** A book from the? What If! creative agency.

3   Barez-Brown, C. (2006). **How to Have Kick-Ass Ideas.** Harper Element.

# DISCERNING

# HOW TO PRIORITISE TASKS READY FOR ACTION

An introduction to the concept of prioritising and how you can learn to do it effectively.

## ● ISN'T IT INTERESTING?

Which one would you go for?

### The power of choice

We are faced with so many different choices each and every day. The coffee shop chain Starbucks has boasted that it offers each customer 19,000 beverage possibilities at every store. Being able to choose what needs to happen and when can help to provide control of a situation. At work we are faced with many choices and therefore countless decisions, and having choices can either help or hinder us. So what are the effects on us of having too much choice?

### Which one do I choose?

In a fascinating study, Kathleen Vohs and her colleagues[1] decided to research the effect of choice on our mental functioning. The researchers asked one group of participants to make choices on some consumer goods to buy or course options to choose. They then asked another group to think about the various different options but not to make any choices. They then tested the participants using a number of measures such as mental arithmetic, physical wellbeing and recovery from setbacks.

They found that those who were asked to make difficult choices that were perceived as requiring lots of mental effort reported lower levels of self-control. This included less physical stamina, reduced persistence in the face of failure, more procrastination and worsened mental arithmetic. They conducted a further study to test these findings and found that amongst a large sample of shoppers, the more (complex) decisions led to a lesser feeling of self-control, adding credence to the first section of the study.

These results suggest that self-regulation, active initiative, and effortful choosing draw on the same psychological resource. Making decisions depletes that resource, which weakens our subsequent capacity for self-control and active initiative.

## This tool can help

Prioritising can help to make sense of the potential choices we can make. The prioritising process is vital to many different aspects of our life and by doing so effectively you can plan ahead with more confidence. This tool is about **how to prioritise tasks ready for action** and introduces you to the concept of prioritising and how you can learn to do it effectively.

# ● HOW TO PRIORITISE

## Why prioritise?

There are too many things to do. There will always be too many things to do. As you progress in your career, the likelihood is that there will usually be far more 'too many things to do'.

I am sure you have heard people say, 'If only there were more hours in the day, then I could get my work done'. But they'd be wrong – if you approach your tasks hoping that somehow the laws of physics will yield to allow you to meet a deadline, then you need to pay attention now!

You are also likely to have heard people say, 'too much to do, not enough time to do it in'. Well, at least these people are a bit more realistic. They know that people in organisations have many things to do, but they still sound as if they're struggling to do everything asked of them, all at once. To be able to cope with the demands placed on you, you need to be able to prioritise.

By the way, if you think you can already prioritise your tasks effectively then you really should have stopped reading this by now – continuing is a low priority for you!

## How to prioritise tasks

There are two key questions to ask yourself when you have tasks to prioritise:

1. **How important is the task?**

   What does 'important' mean? A useful way to look at this is to think about what you get rewarded for in your job. You need to ensure that you focus your efforts on activities that are valued by your organisation and that your role is designed to deal with.

   A common mistake is to focus on tasks you like doing or find easy – but if these aren't the ones for which you are rewarded, then they're less important.

   Importance is all about asking 'what do I want to get from my job?'. If you want to develop specific skills, then tasks requiring them will become important to you. There is also a need to balance tasks at work that we find rewarding and those that will help with our future development.

2. **How urgent is the task?**

   Urgency depends on when the task needs to be completed. Generally, the sooner the deadline, the more urgent the task. Don't fall into the trap of confusing urgency with importance. If you prioritise on the basis of urgency alone, you might not complete other, important tasks.

# ● PRIORITISATION EXERCISE

This exercise helps you put the ideas discussed here into practice.

## Step 1

The first step is to think about importance. To do this you need to think about what you want to achieve from your job. Once you have done this, you need to think about the type of tasks that will help you achieve your objectives. It is important you carry out this step before you prioritise your tasks, otherwise there will be little meaning to the way you prioritise.

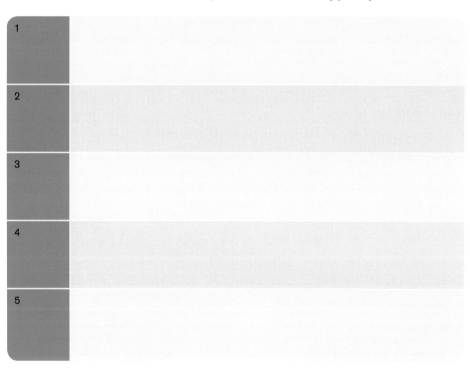

What do I want to achieve from my job?

What are the most important tasks to complete to ensure I meet my job objectives?

| 1 | |
| 2 | |
| 3 | |
| 4 | |
| 5 | |

## Step 2

Once you are clear about what 'importance' means to you, you are ready to prioritise tasks. Using the table on the next page, list some of the tasks you've been asked to complete in the last couple of weeks. Then, rate the importance of each on a scale of 1 to 10, where 10 is 'extremely important'.

Next, consider why they are important. We think some tasks are important just because we do them automatically – but where do they fit on your scale? Again, you might need to think again about what you consider 'important'.

Urgency: Now, rate the urgency of each task on a scale of 1 to 5, where 5 is 'deadline imminent'. (Notice that the 'urgency' scale only goes up to 5 – because your first consideration was to rate a task's 'importance'.)

Priority: Next, add the 'importance' and 'urgency' scores. The tasks with the highest scores are those that you should focus on and do first.

| Task | Importance (1-10) | Why is it important? | Urgency (1-5) | Priority |
|---|---|---|---|---|
| 1 | | | | |
| 2 | | | | |
| 3 | | | | |
| 4 | | | | |
| 5 | | | | |
| 6 | | | | |
| 7 | | | | |
| 8 | | | | |
| 9 | | | | |
| 10 | | | | |

However, this is not the end of the process. As well as prioritising the tasks, you also need to communicate and explain your decisions to those who asked you to do them in the first place! This is, perhaps, a trickier prioritisation skill, because you may need to 'push back' tasks to them. The good news is that going through the process of prioritisation provides you with the justification for telling someone you cannot complete a task they have given you. On your list of tasks are there any you wouldn't have completed – how would you have felt about communicating that?

### Review

So, you have prioritised tasks and decided which ones you cannot complete. Think back over the last couple of weeks – how does this compare with what actually happened?

## ● WHEN TO PRIORITISE TASKS

Prioritising cannot be something you do once a week. Prioritising should be a dynamic process and you should use it whenever you are asked to carry out a task. As you will have seen from the above exercise, your decision to prioritise a task depends on what other tasks you have been asked to complete. Your prioritisation should change as you complete tasks and are invited to do others. Keeping up to date with your task prioritisation will allow you to make decisions as you go.

## Why don't I prioritise my tasks?

From reading through the previous sections you will probably realise that prioritising tasks is not complex, and yet there are many courses available to help people learn to prioritise and manage their time more effectively. In fact, a recent review of academic studies of time management training has concluded:

> Time management behaviours relate positively to perceived control of time, job satisfaction, and health, and negatively to stress. Time management training seems to enhance time management skills, but this does not automatically transfer to better performance.[2]

The research points out the many benefits of being able to manage time effectively, which include job satisfaction and reduced stress – but achieving these benefits doesn't seem so easy! Whilst the skills required to prioritise tasks can be learned, there can be hindrances, or 'blockers' to employing them.

Blockers can be related to our personalities and, therefore, will differ from person to person. Below are some different profiles of people who will find it hard to prioritise.

### Can't Say No

This person cannot say 'no' when asked to do a task. They feel they will be letting people down if they explain they can't do something in the time allowed. This person thinks they are not doing a good job unless they do all they are asked to.

### Starter but not completer

This person enjoys starting new tasks.[3] They get a kick from making some initial early progress, then relax with an assumption that they can finish the task quickly. So reassured, they start the next task.

### The optimist

This person underestimates the time needed to complete tasks and overestimates their capacity for work generally.

### The perfectionist

This person has a need to do all tasks to the best of their ability. So concerned with getting tasks right, they fail to see the importance of each task and over-commit.

### Not enough time to set priorities

This person does not have the luxury of spending time planning and prioritising. They have so many deadlines they don't have time for anything but work.

## ● WHAT TYPE AM I?

Look at these 'blocker' profiles and consider which type you might be. You might even come up with a different type of your own. To do this effectively you need to think in depth about occasions when you have failed to prioritise your tasks effectively and, as a result, failed to meet a deadline.

Describe the situations below:

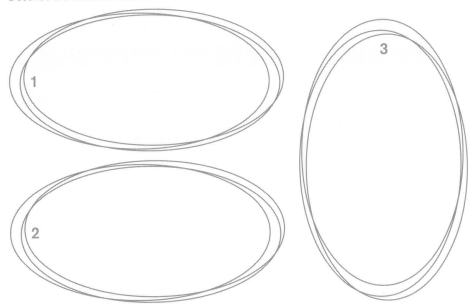

For each of these occasions, ask the questions listed below to think about what went wrong.

| Did you try to prioritise? |
| --- |

**No? Then:**

- Why not?
- What led you to not prioritise your tasks on this occasion?

**Yes? Then:**

- How did you prioritise?
- Did you prioritise the correct task?
- Did you have too many tasks to do?
- Could you have delegated tasks to others?
- Did the task take longer than expected?
- Did you stick to your priorities?
- Finally outline your prioritisation type below.

My prioritisation type is: ...................................................................................................................

## ● MATCH PRIORITY TYPE TO STRATEGY

So, you now know what your prioritisation type is. If you are a 'starter but not a finisher' this final part might be a bit stretching for you, but hang in there! The final part of this tool is to think about strategies you can employ to ensure you prioritise effectively. This will be different for every person.

The table below describes the types and suggested strategies that may help you to prioritise. These are suggested actions only and may not be suitable for you or your work context. In reviewing the strategies below, you can customise your own strategy to help you prioritise.

| Type | Strategy |
|------|----------|
| Can't Say No | You need to stand up for yourself and protect your time. By prioritising and planning your tasks you will be able to offer people evidence as to why you will not be able to do the task they are requesting. |
| The Optimist | You need to engage the help of someone who will be able to provide you with some realism. Plan a prioritisation session with a colleague or secretary once a week. Get this person to make you think about the time required to carry out the tasks you are committing to. |
| The Perfectionist | Re-focus some of your perfectionism onto the prioritisation process. Get this part right and you will be able to carry out your tasks. |
| Not enough time to set priorities | You don't have time to plan because you haven't planned your time. By not setting priorities you will increase your workload as you have no grounds to push back tasks. |
| Starter but not completer | You need to arrange your environment so that you cannot start any other tasks before the current task is complete. For example, go and work in a public library. Take with you only the information you need to complete your task. Stay there until you have finished. |

## ● SUMMARY

When you are under a lot of pressure it's often difficult to manage conflicting pieces of work, let alone know where to start! Consider what the potential de-railer is for your 'type' and the strategies to deal with it. Make sure you choose one (or more) that will work for you. Good luck.

## ● FURTHER INFORMATION

If you found this tool useful then you are likely to find the following tools both insightful and relevant:

- How to make timely decisions
- How to balance risk with potential benefits
- How to deliver every time
- How to take responsibility
- How to formulate action plans.

## ● REFERENCES

1 Vohs, K. et al (2008). Making Choices Impairs Subsequent Self-Control: A Limited-Resource Account of Decision Making, Self-Regulation, and Active Initiative. **Journal of Personality and Social Psychology, 94,** 883–898.

2 Claessens, B., Eerde, W., Rutte, C., & Roe, R. (2007). A Review of the Time Management Literature. **Personnel Review, 36,** 255-276.

3 Lombardo, M. (2004). **For Your Improvement.** Lominger Ltd.

# HOW TO MAKE TIMELY DECISIONS

Increase your awareness of the key elements of decision making, as well as making decisions in a timely manner.

## ● ISN'T IT INTERESTING?

Imagine you're a firefighter in a burning building… it could collapse at any second… you're fighting the flames as you have been trained to… but there is something that strikes you, the way the flame is moving and not responding to your efforts to stop it spreading… how much time do you need to make a decision?

### The Conundrum

The human brain can register information within milliseconds so why do we need so much time to make some decisions, and how can we improve this? Firefighters are required to make quick decisions under pressure like few other professions need to – hesitation can cost lives. But how can you be sure that you are making the right decision?

#### Biases in decision making

We make decisions by gathering information and using our own beliefs and judgement to make these as timely and effective as possible. In order to make our lives easier we use rules of thumb or 'heuristics'[1] to help solve problems, such as applying a specific rule to a range of examples. These guide our judgements and are particularly useful when making quick decisions. However, heuristics can lead to common pitfalls that we need to be aware of and avoid; for example, paying too much attention to the first and last pieces of information or attending to facts we want to whilst ignoring others.

Our thinking processes may be plagued by biases, but they can be hard to identify. This is because the biases are so widespread and natural that they often feel like they fit. So when making decisions think carefully about the information that the judgement is based on in order to avoid being biased.

## This tool can help

It is important to be aware of the factors that influence our decision making in order to prevent them from having a negative impact. This tool is about **how to make timely decisions** and will help you increase awareness of the key elements to decision making as well as helping you make decisions in a timely manner.

# ● FACTORS INFLUENCING DECISION MAKING

There is much involved in leadership, including the ability to think strategically, plan ahead and demonstrate the skills and imagination needed to direct and motivate others. Ultimately, however, assessment of a leader's effectiveness or otherwise depends on the decisions he or she makes.

Most people in business who believe their decision making is logical and rational may be surprised to learn that the process is inevitably affected by personal bias, social and other influences. Did you realise, for example, that you'll make decisions more effectively when you're in a good mood?[2]

Decisions reached by groups are subject to different influences than those made individually. They can benefit from the additional, diverse thought and intelligence available. However, such advantages may also be counteracted by the kinds of social influences which result in conformity, or 'groupthink'.

In the following two sections, we'll describe the most significant ways in which group and individual decision making can be influenced.

# ● INFLUENCES ON INDIVIDUAL DECISION MAKERS

## Personal style

Whether you make your decisions according to your 'gut instinct', or after collecting as much information as possible, this will affect the appropriateness or effectiveness of your decisions. If working as part of a group, it will influence the way you interact with others. Of course, most of us think we 'know' how we do things, but you might be surprised by the result of a personality questionnaire such as the Myers Briggs Type Indicator (MBTI)®, Saville Wave® or Occupational Personality Questionnaire (OPQ)®. If you're interested, get in touch with us.

## Expertise

It's easy to assume that those who know most about an issue are best able to make an effective decision about it, but they're just as likely to spend more time evaluating their information than deciding what to do with it.

## Use of heuristics

Heuristics are 'rules of thumb', educated guesses, intuitive judgements or just 'common sense'. For example: 'Snakes can be dangerous, take care to avoid them'. More precisely, heuristics are simple rules for dealing with all likely outcomes for a particular subject or issue.

People often resort to heuristics, or their previous, limited personal experience as shortcuts through the otherwise complex data necessary to decision making.

Here are some of the biases that affect our decision making most often:

| Common | Biases |
|---|---|
| Illusion of control | Since we're always subject to external factors beyond our control, most of us think we have more control over a given situation that we really do. |
| Overconfidence | Most of us believe we're better (at most things!) than what is statistically calculated as 'average'. So, for example, 85% of us think we're better than average drivers. We make many of our decisions, therefore, without seeking further information beforehand. |
| Confirmatory bias | When we subscribe to a stereotype or form our own belief about something we're quicker to notice what confirms it than what disproves it, even though evidence for and against may exist in equal proportions. |
| Attribution error | We commonly attribute our disappointments and failures to external circumstances, for example: 'The bank's experiencing a credit squeeze, so we didn't get a loan.' But when something goes wrong for others, we'll often assume they're responsible, for example: 'They didn't get a loan because they're not creditworthy'. |
| Availability | We tend to remember and cite the more extreme examples of our own and others' experiences, even if they're not typical. |
| Anchoring | Without realising it, we often base our decisions on a particular belief, assumption, first impression or other 'anchor' of information. |
| Sunk cost trap | We usually decide how much more to invest in a project according to what's already been spent, but that's a 'sunk cost' – future decisions should be based on future potential. |

# ● INFLUENCES ON GROUP DECISION MAKING PROCESSES

## Conformity

Many studies[3] have shown that when in groups, we tend to conform. Two of the most common reasons for this are a) we want to fit in and be liked by the rest of the group, or b) we trust the judgement of others more than our own, in a particular situation.

## Minority Influence

Although commonplace, conformity in groups is not inevitable. Minorities can exert a powerful influence if they show conviction and keep their arguments consistent.[4]

## Obedience

Research[5] reveals we tend to defer to those who are, or seem to be, in a position of authority – and agree to, or do, things we wouldn't otherwise.

## Group Polarisation

Groups can make riskier decisions than their members would, individually. We often mistakenly assume that an idea is substantiated if others agree with it – and can be persuaded to take it further, or to extremes.

## Groupthink[6]

This is an extreme version of 'group polarisation', occurring when a group lacks diversity and dissenting voices. Believing that, because everyone involved thinks alike, decisions reached must be right, the group either doesn't look for evidence to the contrary, or disregards it.

# ● TOOLS TO AID DECISION MAKING

Now you're aware of the possible influences on your decision making ability, we'll suggest three techniques to help counteract some of them – one for when you're on your own, and two for group situations.

## Mind Mapping[7]

This allows you to use your imagination and logic simultaneously, stimulating more of your brain than you might otherwise use at any one time. It helps you consider and evaluate more information relevant to an issue and, therefore, enables a quicker and more effective decision. All you need are some large sheets of paper, several coloured pens and the willingness to try something different!

Start by drawing or writing whatever it is you need to make a decision about in the middle of your sheet of paper. For example, if you're trying to decide whether to launch a new brand, write 'New Brand.' Then, let your thoughts about it flow. For each different or 'key' thought, draw a line or squiggle radiating from the central symbol and write, or draw, the thought along it.

You can use different colours for different branches, or to indicate that they relate to each other. Some or all of the branches might then sprout others, like this:

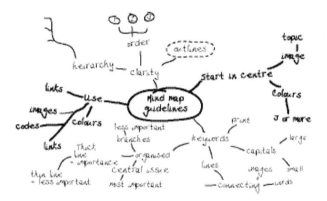

When you feel you've finished your 'mind map' you'll have a picture of all the important and lesser elements relating to the decision. It'll help you see how ideas and actions link up to become meaningful output. You could use it for discussion with others – ask them for comments or to make their own to compare with it, before making a decision.

## Brainstorming

This is used in groups to flush out as many ideas as possible before making a decision – a favourite way is to gather people in a room with a flipchart and to ask them to start throwing out ideas on a given topic, such as: 'Why should we outsource our call centre to India?'

No one should be allowed to express judgements until the brainstorming process is completed. Building on each other's ideas is encouraged and all suggestions – even wild ones – should be recorded.

However, even during brainstorming some of the biases we described earlier, like conformity or groupthink, can surface to inhibit the process, unless very effectively managed. One way to avoid this is to brainstorm electronically, which can yield even better results.

In electronic brainstorming, all contributors type their contributions into a laptop, and they then flash up on a large screen which everyone can see. This means that the contributions are kept anonymous and contributors can build on others' ideas.

When not effectively managed, groups can start judging contributions too early in the process, which may inhibit it. One way to avoid this is 'reverse brainstorming', by asking everyone for reasons why something might not work: 'What could go wrong if we outsourced to India?' This allows contributors to air their concerns about a proposal before discussing how each might be resolved.

It's always important to use a skilled facilitator to ensure brainstorming sessions work effectively, especially when reverse brainstorming, to prevent the negativity dominating proceedings, and the champion of a cause being left feeling under attack!

## Six hat thinking system[8]

This is a way of encouraging lateral thinking using six differently coloured, symbolic hats (the 'hats' could be badges or any other visible marker which individuals could wear or pick up). Each indicates a different way of thinking about something. They should never be used to symbolise individuals, although people could be asked to hold up or wear a particular hat, to indicate the kind of thinking they're adopting, when speaking.

In a group, the hats could be used in a specific sequence or as part of a discussion, where they can be used as required, for example 'I think we should have 5 minutes of "green hat thinking" before taking this discussion further.'

| Six Thinking Hats | |
| --- | --- |
| 1. White hat | Data gathering mode: facts, figures, asking questions, defining informational needs and gaps. |
| 2. Red hat | Intuition and emotions may be expressed without being supported by logic. |
| 3. Black hat | Logical negative, judgement and caution: a very important hat that might need to be used more than others. It's critical that it remains logical. |
| 4. Yellow hat | Logical positive: looks at the value and advantages of an issue or why it has worked previously or elsewhere. |
| 5. Green hat | Provocations, alternatives and creativity. |
| 6. Blue hat | Overview and process control: concerned not with the issue under discussion, but methods and logic. |

In wearing a specific hat, an individual can express thoughts, concerns or feelings as part of the process rather than as personal opinions which he or she feels are vulnerable to judgement by others. It also enables a group to overcome some of the biases we've discussed, and consider an issue from different or unaccustomed perspectives. Here are examples of hats with different attitudes!

1. White hat: Lets see what the facts tell us

2. Red hat: I love the idea of moving to India

3. Black hat: Just because it's cheaper, doesn't mean it's better

4. Yellow hat: XYZ saved a lot of money outsourcing

5. Green hat: Lets move our whole firm to India

6. Blue hat: Let's do some Black Hat thinking

## ● HAVE YOU MADE YOUR MIND UP YET?

This exercise will highlight what's most important in making timely decisions, and help you identify what has or hasn't worked well for you, in your previous experiences.

### Step 1

Think of three, different decision making situations you've experienced: one in which you made a decision too quickly, another when you took too long and a third when it was on time and effective.

### Step 2

Complete our 'Decision making process' template by answering these questions for each of the situations you chose:

- What was the context of the situation?
- What did you have to make a decision about?
- What actions did you take?
- What was the outcome?

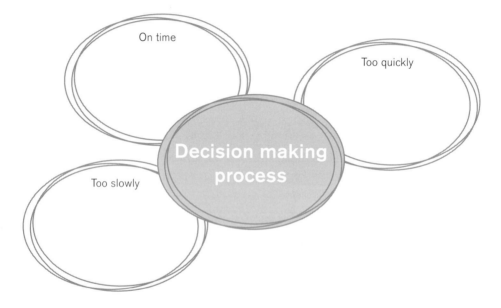

### Step 3

Now, review the scenarios you've just described. It's helpful to reflect on what worked or didn't work and why, in order to learn how to do things differently in future, if necessary. Do this now, by thinking about and answering the following:

- What worked well and why?
- What didn't work well and why?
- What were the consequences of making a decision too quickly?
- What were the consequences of making a decision too slowly?
- What were the key elements to making a timely decision?
- How can I optimise this behaviour again?
- What support do I need to help me make more timely decisions?

Through this exercise you should have identified some of the key factors in helping you to make timely decisions. It is often useful to reflect on past experience in order to learn from mistakes and consider what we could do differently and more successfully in the future and what we should keep on doing which has worked for us in the past.

## ● HINTS AND TIPS FOR TIMELY DECISIONS

- Make sure you have as much available or accessible information as possible.
- Do you need more information – if so, what? Where will you find it?
- Have you consulted relevant stakeholders about who needs the decision, who's involved and what the budget is, if appropriate?
- Agree at the outset when the decision is needed by.
- Keep to the time limit, but try to make your plan flexible to allow for unforeseen circumstances.
- Allocate time for collecting information and consulting people before the decision needs to be made.
- If others are working with you, communicate your plans to everyone involved, so that each knows what needs to be done, and when.
- Brainstorm potential obstacles which could delay or compromise your decision.
- Think about possible objections from others and how you would address them.
- Think about the implications of making your decision too late or too early.
- Prioritise tasks to help ensure a timely decision.
- If you are making a decision in a team, delegate tasks to ensure everyone is involved and all the information is collected in a timely way.

## ● NEXT STEPS

Now that you have considered the information in this tool and tried out some of the practical exercises, here are a number of next steps to embed the learning:

### Look for opportunities to practise

Think about opportunities in your current work, or elsewhere to practise making timely decisions. When do you need to make them by, to suit you and others?

## Talk to a role model

Is there someone you know who is good at making timely decisions? If so, talk to them – they may help you by talking about their own experiences.

## Discuss the 'Have you made your mind up yet?' exercise

Arrange a meeting with three key people; one could be your mentor, the second your line manager and the third a member of your team. Using the 'Have you made your mind up yet?' exercise we described earlier, ask each for feedback under step 3. They'll have different perspectives about your skills and may raise issues you didn't think of when you did the exercise for yourself – all of which will further your development.

Set up another, future meeting and ask the same people if they notice any change in your decision making processes, and anything you could still improve.

## Write a development plan

Make improving these skills a formal objective and include it in your personal development plan, or create one, making this a starting point. Give yourself clear objectives and specific actions to help you make noticeable progress.

Remember that the best way to avoid falling into any of the individual or group decision making biases is to be aware of them: **Forewarned is forearmed.**

# ● FURTHER INFORMATION

If you found this tool useful then you are likely to find the following tools both insightful and relevant:

- How to prioritise tasks ready for action
- How to make ethical decisions
- How to be confident in making judgement calls
- How to balance risk with potential benefits.

# ● REFERENCES

1  Kahneman, D., Tversky, A. & Slovic, P. (eds.) (1982). **Judgement under Uncertainty: Heuristics & Biases.** Cambridge, UK: Cambridge University Press.

2  Cropanzano, R., & Wright, T. (1999). A five-year study of the relationship between wellbeing and performance. **Journal of Consulting Psychology,** 51, 252-265.

3  Asch, S. (1956). Studies of independence and conformity: A minority of one against a unanimous majority. **Psychological Monographs,** 70 (Whole no. 416).

4  Moscovici, S. (1976). **Social influence and social change.** London: Academic Press.

5  Milgram, S. (1963). Behavioral study of obedience. **Journal of Abnormal and Social Psychology,** 67, 371-378.

6  Janis, I. (1972). **Victims of groupthink.** Boston: Houghton-Mifflin.

7  Buzan, T (2006). **The Ultimate Book of Mind Maps.** Harper Thorsons.

8  De Bono, E. (1985) **Six Thinking Hats.** Little, Brown and Company.

# HOW TO FOCUS ON THE BIGGER PICTURE

Raise yourself from the detail in order to focus on the overall context, and help you to be more strategic.

## ● ISN'T IT INTERESTING?

© Aude Oliva and Philippe G Schyns

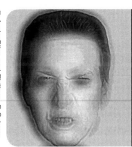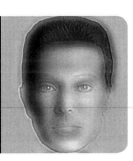

Take a look at the faces in the picture. Are they angry or calm?

### Dr Angry and Mr Smile

The person on the left appears to have a frown and snarl, giving an impression that they are angry. In contrast, the wide eyed person on the right with a hazy focus appears calm and relaxed. Now step back and look at the picture from about 12 feet away. Now, which face is calm and which face is angry? You will notice that they appear to have swapped; the person to the left now looks wide eyed and calm and the one on the right looks like they are frowning and angry! But why is this?

#### Just a matter of perspective?

Depending on the distance you look at this picture from you see something totally different. This diagram, called a hybrid image,[1] was designed to illustrate the ability of the visual system to separate information coming from different spatial frequency channels, i.e. how you perceive the same information at different depths using various parts of the eye and brain.

This change in perspectives often applies to work situations. The decisions, opinions and solutions you choose are likely to differ depending on the perspective from which you view a task or problem. Often, if you take a step back and look at the bigger picture you could come up with a completely different solution than by considering every point in detail.

## This tool can help

As a manager it's a good skill to be able to focus on the bigger picture; to take a more strategic view and not get preoccupied with details. Managers often need to maintain focus on the wider business objectives rather than the details of a task. This tool is about **how to focus on the bigger picture** and provides you with some insight into how to raise yourself from the detail in order to focus on the overall context. This should help you to be more strategic, contextual and visionary.

# ● FOCUSING ON THE BIGGER PICTURE

Focusing on the bigger picture in the workplace is becoming an increasingly valued skill. It is important to focus on the bigger picture to ensure that ideas that are implemented actually tie in with the achievement of your overall objectives. It is easy to get bogged down with the detail and lose sight of what you are actually trying to achieve.

Many people find that their thinking patterns will naturally tend to focus on 'how' without always considering 'why' and 'what'. This focus on processes rather than strategy is sometimes a consequence of the reward system of the organisation. Reward systems tend to be based on processes with less regard for the overall strategy of the organisation. Strategic planning and thinking are necessary at both an organisational and individual level in order to capture the bigger picture.

Strategic thinking involves ascertaining what it is that decides the direction, nature and focus of the business. Strategic planning focuses on how to get there.

### Always ask 'WHY' before 'HOW'

The purpose of asking 'WHY?' before 'HOW?' is to understand the way in which your task fits in with the overall strategy of the organisation. It is vital to question your actions in this way to ensure that you are not wasting your efforts on tasks that are not aligned with either your own goals or the organisation's goals. It is very easy to work hard at something only to find that you are working towards the wrong goal!

In terms of organisational goals it should be quite easy to understand what these are by talking to others in your organisation. If you are focusing on individual goals it can be slightly more complicated. However, there are several techniques you can use. Some examples follow:

## Visualisation

Visualise your ideal self in the future, e.g. Where are you? What are you doing? What have you achieved? This helps to develop a memory trace and understand how you might achieve the goals. This skill takes practice and perseverance, yet many hugely successful individuals swear by it – so it is worth a try.

## Systems thinking

Research indicates that a different technique to help us focus on the bigger picture involves becoming familiar with 'Systems thinking'. This is a framework based on the belief that the only way to fully understand why a problem occurs and persists is to understand the individual part in relation to the whole system. The idea is that component parts of a system are interdependent on the rest of it. If you attempt to isolate a component, then it will behave differently from when it was part of the larger system.

For example, if you are managing on a project team who are working to a tight deadline, working very long hours, all feeling pressurised and feel that deadlines cannot be met, you might conclude that you need to recruit an additional project member to spread the workload. However, taking this narrow approach may mean that you overlook the bigger picture. The project team:

- Have unclear roles and responsibilities
- Are not working efficiently
- Are not sharing information
- Are not motivated to complete the project
- Have a lack of resources.

Recruiting an additional project member will not help to solve the problem, as the other issues need to be addressed.

So, how can we focus on the bigger picture, but in a one-step-at-a-time way? Read on to understand how you can do this.

## Biography

Write your own mini biography as you would like it to be! What would people say about you? What defined you as a person? What were your biggest achievements? This is a very effective way to identify what it is that you really value and want to be remembered for!

## ● TOWS STRATEGIC ALTERNATIVES MATRIX

TOWS is an acronym for Threats, Opportunities, Weaknesses and Strengths. It is based on a SWOT analysis. SWOT traditionally focuses on the internal environment in isolation, whereas TOWS focuses on both internal and external factors.

It is used to generate and classify a person's strategic alternatives in a given situation – to help focus on the bigger picture. Using the TOWS model can help you to widen the number of options you consider rather than only focusing on the immediate options that spring to mind.

The table below provides an outline of the TOWS model:

|  | External Opportunities (O) | External Threats (T) |
|---|---|---|
| Internal Strengths (S) | SO<br>Strategies that **use strengths** to **maximise opportunities** | ST<br>Strategies that **use strengths** to **minimise threats** |
| Internal Weaknesses (W) | WO<br>Strategies that **minimise weaknesses** by **taking advantage of opportunities** | WT<br>Strategies that **minimise weaknesses and avoid threats** |

To use the TOWS model to your best advantage, follow the steps below:

## Step 1

Think of a goal you want to achieve. Consider the information you have relating to your strategic alternatives and conduct a systematic review of this information. This will help you better understand your strengths and weaknesses, as well as identifying your opportunities and threats that you should focus on. Use the grid on the next page to identify and record your strengths, weaknesses, opportunities and threats.

## Step 2

For each grid segment review how you can create good strategic options:[2]

- **Strengths and Opportunities (SO)**
  How might you adopt your strengths to guarantee you take advantage of these opportunities?

- **Strengths and Threats (ST)**
  In what ways might you be able to use your strengths to help you to avoid your actual or possible threats?

- **Weaknesses and Opportunities (WO)**
  How can you adopt your opportunities in a way that will help you to overcome your weaknesses?

- **Weaknesses and Threats (WT)**
  How might you minimise your weaknesses to avoid future threats?

## ● YOUR PERSONAL TOWS GRID

Objective: Complete your project on time and budget and exceed customer expectations

| | External Opportunities (O) | External Threats (T) |
|---|---|---|
| Internal Strengths (S)<br>1.<br>2.<br>3.<br>4.<br>5. | SO<br>Example: 1. External opportunity – changing client needs. Use strength of creative thinking and innovation to come up with exciting new ideas to engage the client. | ST<br>Example: 1. External threat – tight deadline and budget. Use strength of strong organisational skills to project plan effectively and deliver on time and to budget. |
| Internal Weaknesses (W)<br>1.<br>2.<br>3.<br>4.<br>5. | WO<br>Example: 1. One of my team members on the project is excellent at negotiating. I will maximise the opportunity to utilise their skills to negotiate with suppliers to overcome my weaker negotiation skills. | WT<br>Example: 1. I will minimise my weakness in negotiation and avoid future threats in this area by going on a training course to help with negotiation skills. |

Using this grid will help you understand how to focus on the bigger picture. You can use the bigger picture information you generate to evaluate the different options.

It is important to focus on the areas that will give you the greatest benefits. The aim of this tool is to consider your options in a systematic and intelligent manner. It will allow you to look at the strengths or pluses while considering the weaknesses or minuses.

With this knowledge you can move forward more confidently, so why not use the same method with others?

## Broader understanding

This tool will help you gain a much broader understanding of the bigger picture beyond your original beliefs and the result will be a more complete picture.

# ● NEXT STEPS

You should have more of an idea of how to start thinking on a broader level. Here are some suggestions about what to do next, although this list is by no means exhaustive:

## Gather feedback on existing performance

You may find it useful to ask for formal or informal feedback. This may help you to understand how other people perceive you and get advice about where you can make modifications or improvements to think about the wider context. You can also use this information to manage people's future expectations about your approach as well as to monitor your progress.

## Consider a role model

Try and identify someone you know who you admire for their ability to think about the broader context. Think about what it is you like about their approach. This is the starting point for you to develop a plan to improve – see below.

## Look for opportunities to practise

Watch out for opportunities in your current work or elsewhere to practise using the TOWS grid or another approach that will help you to see the bigger picture.

## Write a development plan

Use this tool to write out a personal, focused development plan on how you can best think more broadly.

# ● FURTHER INFORMATION

If you found this tool useful then you are likely to find the following tools both insightful and relevant:

- How to identify your personal meaning
- How to develop strategic long-term goals
- How to make complex ideas simple, clear and concise
- How to make ethical decisions
- How to take responsibility.

# ● REFERENCES

1   Schyns, P. & Oliva, A. (1999). Dr. Angry and Mr. Smile: when categorization flexibly modifies the perception of faces in rapid visual presentations. **Cognition,** 69, 243-265.

2   Ginter, P., Swayne, L. & Duncan, W. (2002). **Strategic Management of Healthcare Organizations.** Blackwell Publishing.

# HOW TO MAKE COMPLEX IDEAS SIMPLE, CLEAR AND CONCISE

Understand how to break complex ideas down into simpler elements and learn about the impact of personal style on how you process complex information.

## ● ISN'T IT INTERESTING?

### What is happening in this picture?

At first glance this picture makes sense. However, when you look in more detail you realise that this is an optical illusion and is actually fairly complex. Our brain initially tries to make sense of the picture but when this is not possible we use techniques such as concentrating on the part that makes sense, squinting or moving away from the picture. How would you explain the picture so someone else could understand what you are looking at?

### It's a set of white dice...

There are a number of explanations that you might give to others. These depend on a number of factors such as which part of the detail you reflect on, how rational you are, what you choose to communicate to people, and how.

You might say, for example:

- The picture is an optical illusion that shows a number of white dice in a triangle shape which looks real but can't be.

- The dice have been manipulated so it looks like two sides are lying flat on the table with the final side standing upright at a 90 degree angle.

- The image doesn't make sense as it doesn't comply with the laws of physics.

When making complex ideas clear and concise you need to engage with your audience, which is dependent on your understanding their needs in order to pitch your message appropriately. If people are familiar with, and able to understand, your concepts then they are more likely to challenge you, which means that your points will require more thought. If people are not familiar with the information they are presented with, or the situation is ambiguous, they are more likely to rely on peripheral characteristics such as your perceived credibility and attractiveness, hence the use of 'attractive' celebrities in advertising.[1]

Richard Saul Wurman defined the concept of an 'information architect'[2] to describe someone who is amongst other things able to 'organize the patterns inherent in data, making the complex clear'. Several reviews have shown that an abundance of this ability is key, especially in modern information-laden companies.

## This tool can help

There are always times when it's difficult to break down a complex idea into simple parts that can be explained more easily. This tool is about **How to make complex ideas simple, clear and concise** and aims to help you understand how to break complex ideas down into simpler elements. The tool explores the impact of personal style on how you process complex information so you understand how others may prefer to use different formats from your own.

## ● COMPLEX THINKING

When Einstein first developed his theory of relativity, only a handful of people in the world could understand it. Now, 100 years later, nearly every physics undergraduate can.

This seems strange, given that the ideas are as complex now as they were 100 years ago. The reason is that physicists have become better at explaining the theory and have had time to conduct practical experiments with it.

Einstein stretched people's minds well beyond contemporary thinking and, let's face it, most of us aren't Einsteins. However, we do have complex ideas we need to explain to others.

There are a number of contexts in which you may need to convey complex ideas. Here we will focus on the two most common:

1. **We have a new idea that we want to explain to others.**
   The people we need to explain an idea to have a similar range of experience or knowledge as ourselves. For example, say you are working in marketing and have just thought of an advertising concept for a product. In your own mind you can see the concept, the images to go with it, the slogans, etc. The challenge is to convey this to your colleagues or a client in a way they can understand it.

2. **We need to convey an idea to someone who is less knowledgeable about the issue.**
   You have to explain complex processes to people who may have only a basic understanding of the subject. For example, a business lecturer explaining the complexities of the stock market to students. Basically, you have something in your head that you need to get across to others, so, consider the following questions:
   - Who is my audience?
   - Is this on a 1:1 basis, in a small group or in a large auditorium filled with people?
   - What method will I use to convey my thinking? Verbal, Written, Graphical or a combination of these methods?

This tool helps you to identify what complex thinking looks like and how to communicate it simply, clearly and concisely.

## ● COMPLEX THINKING MODEL

Making complex ideas simple can be seen as a logical process. You start off with an idea (complex idea/concept), you then have to understand it yourself (defining the elements) and put it into a simple order, to convey it (logical hierarchy established). You then need to consider who you are putting the idea across to (define audience) and your approach (select and implement communications channel).

Of course, this does not always work – there often comes a time in the process where information needs to be reviewed and put forward in a different way, to make it appear simpler for the audience (the feedback loop). As shown in the model, this tends to happen when you convey your idea. You may have to go through this stage a number of times in order to reach the final point where you get the idea across (audience understands).

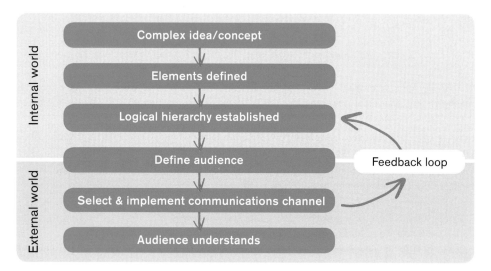

## ● ANYONE FOR CHARADES?

Have you ever played Charades, Pictionary or a similar game? How frustrating is it when your audience are just not getting your very obvious actions or the things you're drawing? They can't follow the logic in your head. These games work on the basis of making simple things complex by imposing restrictions. By understanding this process you can reverse it to make complex things simple.

To make simple things complex we often do the following:

● Remove the ability to name/label things

● Impose time constraints

● Restrict the communication channels we use

● Encourage our audience to interrupt/pressure us

● Restrict non-verbal communications, e.g. pointing, nodding, etc.

So, how can this be used in reverse?

1. **Name and label things to get a common frame of reference** and ensure people have a common understanding of these as you move through your explanation. Be consistent in this and check you're being understood.

2. **Do not put yourself under time pressure** when trying to explain complex issues. They take time, so create the time. Plan your use of the time effectively.

3. **Use as wide a range of communication channels** as you can. Try to use the communication channel that best meets the needs of the audience. For example, if your audience really like to picture things then consider using a PowerPoint presentation with slides of visual images.

4. **Control your audience.** Set rules for how you want them to interact with you. Check that they understand your thinking and give them rules for asking questions or interrupting if they don't understand.

5. **Use non-verbal communications** to check if others understand your points. Are they looking bored or lost? Use your non-verbal skills such as eye contact, gestures, etc. to support and emphasise key points.

## ● PREFERENCES IN GIVING AND RECEIVING INFORMATION

The Myers Briggs Type Indicator (MBTI)®3 personality profile is one way to consider how we like to give information to others and how they like to receive it.

If you already know your MBTI, then skip to the next section, which is all about applying your MBTI type. If not, have a look at the following exercises.

There are 4 dimensions on the MBTI (Extraversion-Intraversion (E-I), Sensing-Intuition (S-N), Thinking-Feeling (T-F) and Judging-Perceiving (J-P)). Each dimension has two sides and a person selects the profile they consider most like themselves. For example, if you feel you're someone who prefers information that's real and tangible, then you are likely to be Sensing (S). The MBTI dimension most relevant to complex thinking is S (Sensing) and N (Intuition).

Read the descriptors below and select whether you are more S or more N. You may feel that you have characteristics from both but select the one that, on balance, is most like you.

| Sensing | Intuition |
|---|---|
| ● Focused on the present | ● Oriented to future possibilities |
| ● Factual and concrete | ● Imaginative and verbally creative |
| ● Focus on what is real and actual | ● Focus on patterns and meanings in data |
| ● Observe and remember details | ● Remember details when they relate to a pattern |
| ● Build carefully and thoroughly towards conclusions | ● Move quickly to conclusions, follow hunches |
| ● Understand ideas and theories through practical applications | ● Want to clarify ideas and theories before putting them into practice |
| ● Trust experience | ● Trust inspiration |

## ● SENSORY OR INTUITIVE?

Do you feel you are sensory or intuitive? Those who favour a sensing (S) approach will search for extra data using their senses to come to a decision, whereas those who prefer intuition (N) are more likely to 'go with their gut'.

It can be helpful to remember that if you are an S then there may be issues when presenting information to an N and vice versa. If you are an N communicating to somebody with an S preference, then you need to take more time over the details. If you have an S preference communicating to an N you need to take more time to think of the 'big picture' first – sell them the concept and then show the detail. Use the information in the table below to help guide the way you present information to S and Ns.

| Sensing | Intuition |
| --- | --- |
| ● Likes evidence and facts | ● Likes broad issues first |
| ● Wants practical applications shown | ● Wants possible future challenges discussed |
| ● Relies on experience and anecdotes | ● Relies on insights and imagination |
| ● Likes feasible suggestions | ● Likes novel suggestions |
| ● Meetings: follows agenda | ● Meetings: uses agenda as starting point |

In looking at the differences between the styles, S can find N types impractical and difficult to follow, while N can find S types pessimistic and overly focused on details.

## ● WRITTEN REPORT EXERCISE

This exercise will help you identify what the crucial points of your idea are, so that you can convey them simply, without being hampered by unnecessary details.

Think about an area of your work that involves complex ideas. Develop a written report to explain this to someone who is new to your area of work, maybe as part of their induction. Ask someone with less experience to review it and see if it makes sense to them. Use the following headings to help you:

● Label/Name the issue (short heading)

● Define, in no more than 15 words, what it is

● Identify the key elements, number them and put them in sequence of understanding, i.e. which concept does the person need to be familiar with in the first instance, then the next concept, etc.

Set out the elements and describe each one in no more than 15 words.

| Element | Definition |
|---|---|
|  |  |
|  |  |
|  |  |
|  |  |

## ● COMMUNICATING COMPLEX THINKING

### The channel to audience matrix

Use the following table to consider your approach to communicating complex ideas in various individual or group situations. It is worth working out which is your preferred approach in order to build on that.

| Situation | 1:1 | Small Group | Large Group |
|---|---|---|---|
| Face to Face | Very good method – allows for non-verbal feedback as well as verbal. You can use this method to check understanding and to allow the person to ask questions, etc. | Effective method and can be supported by prior emails/reports to allow the group to prepare. Important to set ground rules to control how your audience can interact with you in terms of questions, etc. A short PowerPoint-type presentation can be very effective to support this. | Call the meeting in a place where you can set out a clear presentation. Remember your audience is likely to be a mixture of S and N types. Start with the big picture concept before moving on to explain details, to cater for both types. Use graphics to illustrate your concepts and tables/graphs for the finer detail. Control of your audience is essential here and you should definitely regulate questions. Use of follow-up feedback surveys can help to assess the impact of your ideas. |

| Situation | 1:1 | Small Group | Large Group |
|---|---|---|---|
| **Report** | If well laid out in stages, can be effective – depends on individual preferences for assimilating information in this way. For example, Introverts (1 on MBTI), like to receive information in this way, to reflect on it. | As per 1:1. | Limited effectiveness and not practical. |
| **Email** | Poor – may be useful for short simple ideas or follow-on explanations. | Poor as per 1:1. | Not effective. |
| **Video Conference** | Good method if link is effective and allows genuine sharing of information. | Limited. The key problem is allowing people to raise questions. | Very limited – really only for presenting to a group rather than getting feedback from it. |
| **Telephone** | Limited to verbal rather than non-verbal feedback. Can be difficult to retain the other person's interest. | Not effective – limited verbal feedback and no non-verbal feedback. | Not effective. |
| Graphical | Usually used in conjunction with other methods. In face-to-face communications, can enable drawing concepts on paper as you go through the ideas and the use of flow charts, etc., to present information in a step-by-step manner. | Flipcharts are very useful in small groups to allow you to set out your thoughts on paper and develop concepts with others. | Very useful – but don't try to 'draw as you go' with larger groups. Graphics need to be prepared in advance and made suitable for large screen presentation. |

## Summary

The best ideas are often the simplest and you now have strategies for simplifying even the most complicated concepts. You will also have a better understanding of your own preferred ways of assimilating and communicating complicated information simply, clearly and concisely.

## ● NEXT STEPS

You should by now have more of a sense of how to make complex ideas and problems more simple and manageable. Here are some suggestions about what to do next, although this list is by no means exhaustive:

### Gather feedback on existing performance

You may find it useful to ask for formal or informal feedback. This may help you to understand how other people perceive you and get advice about where you can make modifications or improvements. You can also use this information to manage people's future expectations about your approach as well as to monitor your progress.

## Consider a role model

Try and identify someone you know who you admire for their ability to break difficult things down into easy manageable parts. Think about what it is you like about their approach and what works well for them. Then consider how you can adapt your style. This is the starting point for you to develop a plan to improve — see below.

## Look for opportunities to practise

Watch out for opportunities in your current work or elsewhere to practise taking something complex and trying to simplify the problem using the information you have picked up from this tool.

## Write a development plan

Use this tool to write out a personal, focused development plan on how you will make complex things more simple.

## ● FURTHER INFORMATION

If you found this tool useful then you are likely to find the following tools both insightful and relevant:

- How to reframe problems
- How to prioritise tasks ready for action
- How to formulate action plans
- How to communicate your vision.

## ● REFERENCES

1   der Waldt, V., la Rey, D., De Beer, N., & Du Plessis, N. (2007). Attitudes towards attractive and credible celebrities in advertisements: a survey amongst students.

2   Wurman, R. S. (1997). What's an Information Architect?.

3   Myers, I. B. (1962). The Myers-Briggs type indicator. Palo Alto, CA: Consulting Psychologists Press.

4   http://www.sempervitainstitute.com/2012/01/s-to-n-thats-not-data-.html

# HOW TO MAKE ETHICAL DECISIONS

Understand how ethics can directly impact business performance. Key sources of ethical standards are highlighted, providing a framework for making ethical decisions.

## ● ISN'T IT INTERESTING?

Ethics. Standards of right and wrong. Rules. Guidelines suggesting what you ought to do. It seems straightforward. And yet, ask people from different cultures and backgrounds what an ethical decision actually means and you could hear some very different judgements.

### How do we make ethical decisions?

Sometimes the issues we face are not clearly black or white, so we have to make a judgement call. Research conducted into ethical decision making has revealed some fascinating cross-cultural differences.

#### A bribe or incentive?

In 2004, researchers[1] examining culture and ethics analysed data from the World Values Survey databank. They looked at the responses of 3,450 managers from 28 different countries to justify ethically suspect behaviours, such as whether to accept bribes in the course of working duties.

Their analysis pointed to several factors that were predictive of accepting suspect behaviours. For individuals, youth and rejection of religion were the strongest predictors; at a national level, poor schooling and high industrialisation were strongest. They further tested these predictors and identified that many students from 'collectivist' societies (i.e. those cultures in which identity is more strongly defined by long-lasting group membership) were far more willing to offer and accept bribes, as this was part of 'oiling the wheels' of long-term working relationships and being part of an established group.

So while some cultures frown heavily on payments in the form of bribes, others may see them as a natural and regular process in establishing working partnerships. So who is less or more 'ethical' in approach?

## This tool can help

The above example shows how decisions can be driven by different ethical standards, the impact of which can be extremely important in the business world. This tool is about **how to make ethical decisions** and aims to help you understand how ethics can directly impact business performance. The key sources of ethical standards are highlighted so they can be used as a framework for you when making ethical decisions.

## ● WHAT'S ALL THE FUSS ABOUT?

Each and every one of us makes hundreds of decisions every day. From mulling over important decisions about company strategy and operations to agonising over what to have for lunch – we have all developed our own tried and tested methods for deciding what or how to do things.

### So, why should making ethical decisions be any different?

Well, in a nutshell, it's not! Many of the cognitive processes we use to make 'everyday' decisions can also be applied to making decisions with ethical consequences.[2] However, a little extra knowledge can go a long way and this tool will help you to understand the ethical implications of your decisions in more detail and help you make those choices where 'doing the right thing' is of utmost importance.

### What are ethics?

Before we begin, it is important to clarify what we mean by 'ethics'. Ethics are codes of 'good' behaviour in terms of moral duty and obligation. Applied to business, they underpin the guiding principles of culture and behaviour.

Ethical behaviour in business is critical. Over recent years, several high-profile scandals have demonstrated the importance of making ethical decisions. Consider companies such as Enron, WorldCom and Barings Bank, all of which have been involved in financial scandal to one degree or another as a direct result of a series of unethical decisions made by those in positions of authority and power. It may sound a little 'over the top', but these allegations, and others like them, raise concerns about the moral fibre of companies and potentially threaten the nature of the free market economy.

Taking a less extreme view, the ethical foundations for your decisions can play a significant role in business success. For example, you may be faced with the dilemma of using cheap foreign labour in response to price competition. On the one hand, the use of cheap labour will allow you to retain your competitive edge and survive in the marketplace, reducing the need for redundancies. However, on the other hand, the use of cheap labour may be morally wrong and help to drive down wages within the industry.

So, making ethical decisions – not just about 'doing the right thing' and avoiding the courts – is about weighing up the ethical consequences of different actions and using your judgement to reach a decision. Read on to learn more about making ethical decisions.

## ● DIFFERENT APPROACHES TO ETHICAL DECISIONS

It is important to note that ethics are not based on feelings, religion, law, accepted social practice or science. Philosophers and ethicists have been debating the basis of ethics since Socrates suggested that people will naturally do what is good, if they are aware of what is right. Since then, philosophy has broadly condensed the basis of ethical decisions into five different approaches, each of which should be considered when making a decision.

## ● A GUIDE TO ETHICAL DECISIONS

As you will have noted from the previous section, some approaches to ethical decision making are more appropriate in some situations than others.

Clearly, making ethical decisions is no easy task. In our complex global business climate, there are many factors to consider before we can arrive at a decision that not only makes sound business sense but also gives careful consideration to what is morally and ethically 'right'.

The guide below will help you to make such decisions, and incorporates some of the key aspects of the five approaches illustrated above.

Discover the problem

- Is there an ethical dimension to this decision?
- Is there a moral side to be considered?
- If so, who is this decision going to impact on?

Get the relevant info

- What are the relevant facts? What facts are unknown?
- Who is involved in your decision? Have you consulted them?
- Is there a precedent for this action that needs considering?

Make your own judgement

- How do you feel about the issue?
- Do you have a 'gut' feeling one way or the other that you think is valid?

Take a decision and put your plan into action

- Having gathered the information you need, make your decision.
- Draw up a plan of action that you can stick to.
- Be decisive; if it's the right thing to do, then you need to act accordingly with confidence.

Consolidate

- Was everyone happy with your decision?
- Did it have the correct/intended outcome?
- Is there anybody you need to discuss your decision with?

By using this guide, you should be able to formulate some effective and ethical decisions. You may want to practise by designing a hypothetical situation first and trying to come up with an ethical solution using this guide.

Following a guide such as this one is also a way of reducing 'risk'. If a clear plan is not followed, an action which may appear to be ethical may not be correctly implemented. Research has indicated this is a likely cause for many high-profile unethical decisions in large businesses.[3]

## ● BAD CHOICE DETECTORS

If you are still undecided about the ethical course of action, keep some of the following questions on hand as ethical 'smoke detectors'. If alarm bells start ringing in your head once the question is asked, then it is likely that you are not proceeding down the most ethical path. It is, perhaps, a good time to revisit the PK guide to ethical decisions on page 74.

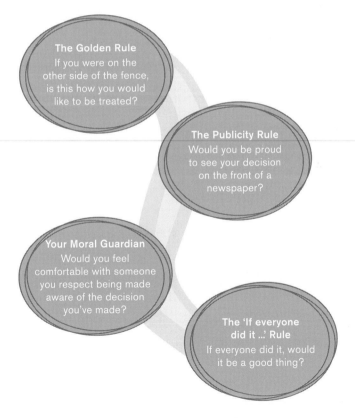

**The Golden Rule**
If you were on the other side of the fence, is this how you would like to be treated?

**The Publicity Rule**
Would you be proud to see your decision on the front of a newspaper?

**Your Moral Guardian**
Would you feel comfortable with someone you respect being made aware of the decision you've made?

**The 'If everyone did it ...' Rule**
If everyone did it, would it be a good thing?

## Integrity

Think about how important it is to show integrity in your work. Whilst sometimes it may be tempting to cut corners it is this ethical dilemma that you should consider — in the long run what is the right thing to do...

## ● NEXT STEPS

Now that you have considered the information in this tool and tried out some of the practical exercises around making ethical decisions, here are a number of next steps to embed the learning:

### Gain feedback

Present your decision making rationale to a colleague or trusted advisor and ask for feedback. Ask that person(s) to be honest and open and review your decision against the bad choice detectors. Are there any flaws and/or different opportunities they can identify for you to incorporate in your decision making?

### Look for opportunities to practise

Think about the opportunities that you have in your current work, or beyond, where you can practise making an ethical decision. Look at your next decision and how you go about thinking ethically. Consider how you can approach the decision, what are the broader implications of your choices, who could be most impacted by the decision? Think about the bad choice detectors when you are making your decision.

### Talk to your role model

Identify someone who you think always behaves ethically and ask them how they go about making decisions. They may be able to provide you with some advice that can help you to be more effective.

### Use the guide on page 74 next time you make a decision

This guide should provide you with a framework to help you to make an ethical decision. Try this approach and see how it works for you.

### Write a development plan

Try forming an objective around making ethical decisions and factor this into your personal development plan, or create one using this as a starting point. Ensure that you give yourself clear objectives and tangible actions that will help you to progress and make a real improvement.

## ● FURTHER INFORMATION

If you found this tool useful then you are likely to find the following tools both insightful and relevant:

- How to make timely decisions
- How to focus on the bigger picture
- How to balance risk with potential benefits
- How to formulate action plans.

## ● REFERENCES

1   Cullen, J., Parboteeah, K. & Hoegl, M. (2004). Cross-national differences in managers' willingness to justify ethically suspect behaviours: A test of institutional anomie theory. **Academy of Management Journal,** 47, 41-21.

2   Rogerson, M. D., Gottlieb, M. C., Handelsman, M. M., Knapp, S. & Younggren, J. (2011). Nonrational processes in ethical decision making. **American Psychologist,** 66(7), 614.

3   Messick, D. M. & Bazerman, M. H. (1996). Ethical leadership and the psychology of decision making. **Sloan Management Review,** 37, 9-22.

# SHAPING

# HOW TO MAKE REASONED JUDGEMENTS

Learn how to develop your judgement-forming skills and apply them in a range of situations.

## ● ISN'T IT INTERESTING?

Ah...isn't he cute?

### But why do you think this baby is attractive?

Attractiveness is subjective, but there are some people (and other things) that nearly everyone finds beautiful. Babies are a good example of this point. People tend to look for symmetry in faces as this is meant to imply strong genes and hence someone who is fit and healthy. The golden ratio, (phi 1:1.618[1]), when present, has been shown to equate to increased beauty. Whether you believe in the golden ratio or not, you are merely trying to short cut the information to make an informed judgement. However, relying on this data can skew your judgement.

### Objective decisions?

Research indicates that many people are influenced by factors in the environment when decision making. A person's physical attractiveness can have an impact on whether we decide to accept or reject their argument:

- A number of studies[2] have shown that people who are attractive tend to have faces that more closely resemble that of babies. For example, they have rounder faces, and their eyes are wider apart than the average.

- Physical attractiveness has been shown to be perceived to link with character and can make individuals be seen as more persuasive. Research[3] has found that people on trial who were rated as attractive were less likely to be found guilty or received shorter sentences than those perceived to be less attractive.

- Attractive people are often perceived as more intelligent, better adjusted, and more popular. This is known as the halo effect.[4] Research shows attractive people also have more occupational success and more dating experience than unattractive people.[5] It could be, however, that higher self-confidence coupled with positive feedback equates to more success.

## This tool can help

We may not like to think that something like physical attractiveness affects our judgement. However, the reality is that it is likely to have at some point. This tool is about **how to make reasoned judgements** and aims to help you make decisions more effectively. The tool guides you in developing your judgement-forming skills and applying them in a range of situations.

## ● WHY IS REASONED JUDGEMENT IMPORTANT?

Reasoned judgement is the process of using all of the available information to weigh the pros and cons of a number of alternative options, leading to a selected course of action.

All reasoned judgements should lead to a final choice. The process begins when we are first aware of the need to take action but are unsure of the best choice. We therefore start the process of reasoned judgement, which is based on both explicit and implicit assumptions.

Reasoned judgement involves a process and an output. This means that part of reasoned judgement will involve a thinking process and part will involve actions that are observable by others. Based on observable actions, we assume that a person has made a commitment to effect the action.

Reasoned judgement plays an important part in many professions, where specialists are required to apply their knowledge to make informed decisions.

## ● A MODEL OF REASONED JUDGEMENT MAKING

When you demonstrate effective judgement, you are doing no more than making rational, realistic and sound decisions based on consideration of all the facts and alternatives available. The model below shows a series of stages we go through when making reasoned judgements.

Model of Rational Judgement[6]

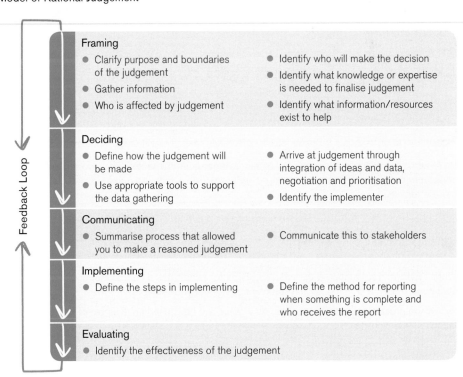

## ● REASONED JUDGEMENT MAKING EXERCISE

Consider three past decisions that you subsequently had to alter. Using the model of reasoned judgement, identify the factors that you did not pay sufficient attention to at the time that could have helped you to come to a better decision. What are the implications for your decision making process?

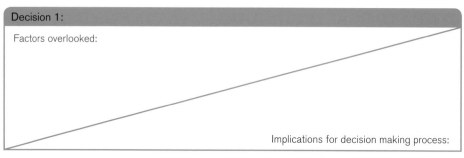

Decision 1:

Factors overlooked:

Implications for decision making process:

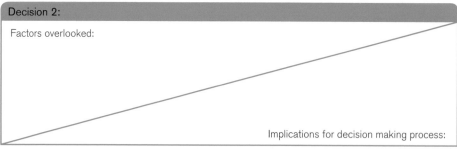

Decision 2:

Factors overlooked:

Implications for decision making process:

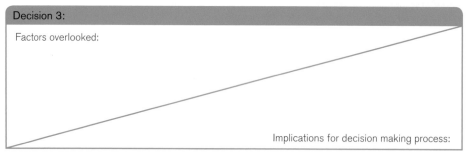

Decision 3:

Factors overlooked:

Implications for decision making process:

Look across your three examples for common themes in the factors you overlooked and their implications. Consider what you could do differently next time, to make your decision making more effective.

## ● CRITERIA MATRIX

When faced with a situation with multiple options for action, use a criteria matrix (such as the one shown) to evaluate which potential solutions best meet your objectives.

Follow the procedure on the next page. As a guide, we have used an example of deciding how to launch a new website.

## Procedure

### Step one

Brainstorm the evaluation criteria appropriate to the situation. If possible, involve customers/ clients in this process.

> **Example:** Cost, time, branding, technology, ease of use, access to information, disability consideration, content, audience, languages.

### Step two

Discuss and refine the list of criteria. Identify any criteria that must be included and any that must not be included. Reduce the list of criteria to those that the team believes are most important.

> **Example:** Most important – Cost, ease of use, content, technology, audience.

### Step three

Based on how important each criterion is to the situation, rate them on a scale of 1-5, 5 being the most important. Remember, you can have more than one criterion with the same rating. The assignment can be done by discussion and consensus or each member can assign ratings. Then, the numbers for each criterion are added for a composite team rating.

> **Example:** Cost = 4, ease of use = 4, content = 3, technology = 1, audience = 5.

### Step four

Consider up to four options to solve your problem.

Option A – Write the website to include your content.

Option B – Conduct market research to find out who the audience are and what they want.

Option C – Test out different technology.

Option D – Have a look at your current website to see what needs to be improved.

Draw a matrix as below, using your own criteria as headings in order of importance.

| Criteria | Option A | Option B | Option C | Option D |
|----------|----------|----------|----------|----------|
| Audience |  |  |  |  |
| Cost |  |  |  |  |
| Ease of use |  |  |  |  |
| Content |  |  |  |  |
| Technology |  |  |  |  |

## Step Five

Evaluate each option against the criteria. If it meets the criterion put a 4. If it does not, put an 8. Choose your preferred option, based on the number of 4s against your criteria. Remember, you have placed more importance on some criteria than others.

## ● NEXT STEPS

- Consider instances where you have procrastinated in making a decision. Identify the factors that made it difficult for you to make a timely and clear choice, and consider what steps you should have taken to reduce your anxiety or reluctance to decide.
- Try using the techniques identified in the tool next time you need to make a reasoned judgement.
- Think about good judgements you have made. What made it go well? Use this information to utilise your strengths next time you make a reasoned judgement.
- Ask others you have worked with recently for feedback to gauge their perceptions on your judgement making process.

## ● FURTHER INFORMATION

If you found this tool useful then you are likely to find the following tools both insightful and relevant:

- How to make timely decisions
- How to focus on the bigger picture
- How to make ethical decisions
- How to balance risk with potential benefits
- How to know when and how to take risks.

## ● REFERENCES

1   Livio, M. (2002). **The Golden Ratio: The Story of Phi, The World's Most Astonishing Number.** New York: Broadway Books.

2   Zebrowitz, L. (1997). **Reading Faces: Window to the Soul?** Boulder, CO, USA: Westviewpress.

3   Darby, B. & Jeffers, D. (1988.) The Effects of Defendant and Juror Attractiveness on Simulated Courtroom Trial Decisions. Social Behaviour and Personality, 16(1), p39-50.

4   Asch, S. (1946). Forming impressions of personality. **Journal of Abnormal and Social Psychology,** 41, 258-290.

5   Aronson, E. (1999). **The Social Animal.** New York: Worth Publishers, Inc.

6   Scholtes, P., Joiner, B. & Streibel, B. (2003). **The Team Handbook (3rd edition).** OrielPAGE.

# HOW TO DIRECT PEOPLE

Understand the concepts of 'discretionary effort' and 'engagement'.

## ● ISN'T IT INTERESTING?

The red cross on white background was the original protection symbol declared at the 1864 Geneva Convention:

### Getting others on board

The International Red Cross stands as an impartial, neutral and independent organisation for the protection of the life and dignity of victims of international and internal armed conflicts. With over 96 million members worldwide it is a huge job to get people to meet these needs. So how do you get people to work towards a shared goal? Psychologists would point you to social influence theory[1] to explain how people can be persuaded and influenced. Principally, social influence is changing someone's behaviour, intentionally or unintentionally, based on how the changed person perceives the influencer, other people or society in general. There are three areas of social influence: conformity, compliance and obedience. Conformity is changing how you behave to be more like others; compliance is when a person does something that they are asked to do by another; and obedience is obeying an order from someone you accept as an authority figure. The research example below shows one method of persuading others.

### The best request

During a research project,[2] participants were given two requests with the direct intention of one being rejected but by doing so making the other request more desirable. The researchers asked the participants to give one pint of blood either the following day, or every six weeks for the next year. The students rejected the latter request but then when asked to give blood the following day they were much more likely to do so.

The researchers felt that this was due to the contrast effect, where an extreme request makes a lesser request more reasonable. People were also more likely to agree if the initial request was withdrawn, as it seemed to make individuals feel that they should give something back in return (e.g. by giving blood the next day).

## This tool can help

Individuals can be persuaded to go that extra mile and do something for nothing. However, encouraging this in others can be tricky. This tool is about **how to direct people** and will introduce you to the concept of 'discretionary effort' which is the amount of effort we are willing to put into the work we do, over and above what is required. This is closely linked with an individual's engagement and this tool will help you to explore your style and how you can adapt this to encourage these behaviours in others.

# ● UNDERSTANDING DISCRETIONARY EFFORT

## Directing people to meet organisational goals

An organisation is only as good as its people. True – but it's more about how managers direct and maximise the potential of those people. Getting people to achieve organisational goals is one thing, but wouldn't it feel good – and profitable – if this and more was achieved because everyone felt motivated to give just a little extra? So, here we'll take a slightly different perspective from most other advice offered to managers. This is about the difference 'discretionary effort' and 'employee engagement' make to what and how things are achieved.

## What is discretionary effort?[3]

It's when people choose to contribute more than is required to meet minimum standards of performance. Discretionary effort (DE) is about giving more than is itemised on a job description, or demanded by specific targets. It's not necessarily about working longer hours but includes, for example:

- Helping a busy colleague with their workload
- Volunteering to run or take part in activities either within the organisation or on its behalf
- Suggesting or developing improvements and alternatives to existing practices and products.

## How is discretionary effort going to help me?

Research suggests that in an environment where DE is encouraged and recognised, employees are not only more efficient and productive, but demonstrate greater 'engagement'. These two, interdependent characteristics are what drive the most successful organisations. In other words, when people are made to feel they belong, with value and potential beyond their mere function, they give more.

If that sounds like the kind of white noise you'd expect from a bunch of psychologists who aren't sandwiched, like you, between a remote executive and all the cynical, clock-watching wage slaves you manage, then here are some stats you can bite on:

Results from the Gallup Workforce Studies[4] revealed, during a fixed time period, that the bottom line in those organisations whose employees demonstrated the two dynamics we've been discussing was improved as a result of increasing operating and net profit margins. Those without it showed a decline in these financial indicators during the same period. More specifically, organisations that adopted a deliberately inclusive approach to encourage DE experienced:

- Greater customer satisfaction/loyalty + 39%
- Increased productivity + 22%
- Higher profitability + 27%
- Lower turnover – 22%.

# ● INCREASING DISCRETIONARY EFFORT

There are three requirements for encouraging DE in the workplace, concerning managerial activities, organisational environment and diversity issues. The way these are related is demonstrated like this:

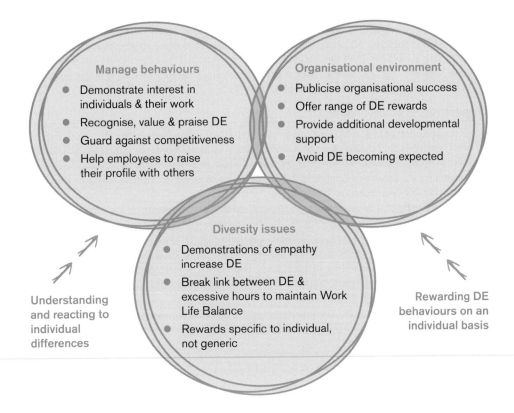

Understanding and reacting to individual differences

Rewarding DE behaviours on an individual basis

**Manage behaviours**
- Demonstrate interest in individuals & their work
- Recognise, value & praise DE
- Guard against competitiveness
- Help employees to raise their profile with others

**Organisational environment**
- Publicise organisational success
- Offer range of DE rewards
- Provide additional developmental support
- Avoid DE becoming expected

**Diversity issues**
- Demonstrations of empathy increase DE
- Break link between DE & excessive hours to maintain Work Life Balance
- Rewards specific to individual, not generic

Here are some things you need to do encourage DE in your workplace. You may already do some of them, but you could start thinking about those you hadn't considered, until now:

## Manage behaviours:

- Openly recognise, praise and value any DE behaviour your team shows.
- Give positive feedback to your team.
- Show interest in individual team members and their work (even before seeing any evidence of DE).
- Employees will demonstrate DE if it raises their profile with others. As well as personally recognising someone's effort, tell other managers about it, if appropriate, and ask them to acknowledge the individual, too.
- Talk about or demonstrate how instances of individual DE have contributed to team or organisational successes. This helps the individual concerned and the rest of the team understand its overall impact – and can even channel competitiveness more constructively, by demonstrating how everyone benefits.

## Diversity issues

Employees offer more DE if those around them are empathic. This means you need to develop the following skills:

- Make it clear you're listening when an employee is talking to you.
- Show you can see things from the employee's perspective.
- Show you care during difficult times.
- Take care that employees don't think you're encouraging excessive workloads or longer hours. Make sure you 'showcase' examples which haven't involved staying at work longer, but if this is the case, then ensure people know the individual has been given leave in lieu.
- Give different kinds of reward, which make it clear you've thought about the tastes and preferences of the individuals concerned.

## Organisational environment

- Employees demonstrate more DE when they feel proud of the organisation for which they work. Activities that publicise organisational (global or local) and team successes are key to increasing DE – because this increases morale, which in turn contributes to DE.
- Rewarding DE behaviour is important, but this needs to be done carefully. Rewards should not be predictable, or always financial.
- Give developmental support. Many employees report that their discretionary efforts are to develop their own skills, so building on this will increase motivation.

Critically, employees must never be given the impression that DE is expected of them. DE should remain exactly what it is – discretionary – and the key message should remain that DE is about recognition, not expectation. This is particularly important because employees will assume it involves working additional hours. It is essential to get the balance right – be seen to be as much of an advocate of 'work-life balance' as of DE.

Discretionary effort can be elusive, but those most likely to demonstrate it are those who are 'engaged', which is what we're going to explain next…

# ● UNDERSTANDING ENGAGEMENT

## What is engagement?[5]

Engagement is a measure of an employee's emotional and intellectual commitment to their organisation and its success. It describes how employees behave as a result of their interactions with the organisation; that is, their involvement, contribution and ownership.

It's a positive attitude employees have towards the organisation and its values. An 'engaged' employee is aware of business context, and consciously works to improve the organisation's performance. Importantly, it's a two-way process; organisations must work to engage the employee, who must be allowed choice about his or her level of engagement.

## How is engagement going to help me?

Research suggests that engaged employees show the following:

- A belief in the organisation
- A desire to work to make things better
- An understanding of the business context and the 'bigger picture'
- Respect and support for colleagues
- A willingness to keep up to date with developments in the field
- Higher levels of job satisfaction
- Higher levels of organisational commitment
- More likely to engage in organisational citizenship behaviours.

Research has also found that engagement has a direct impact on business outcomes.[6] Engaged employees have been found to:

- Deliver better customer satisfaction
- Positively influence customer loyalty ratings
- Improve financial out-turn
- Show low levels levels of employee turnover.

## ● IMPROVING ENGAGEMENT

Research by the Institute for Employment Studies (IES) found that what produces engagement more than anything else, is a sense of feeling valued and involved. For this, people need to:

- Be involved in decision making
- Feel able to voice their ideas. Managers must listen to these views and value employees' contributions
- Have opportunities to develop within the organisation
- Feel that the organisation is concerned for their health and wellbeing.

Line managers play a vital role in fostering a sense of value and involvement through conducting performance appraisals, communicating with team members and other employees, identifying training opportunities and ensuring equality of opportunity.

The IES found that feeling valued and involved at work is also linked to availability of training and development, the attitude and behaviour of managers, the manner of appraisals, communication, equal opportunities and fair treatment.

Here is a model of 'engagement' devised by the IES, based on its most important contributors, which are 'feeling valued' and 'involved'.

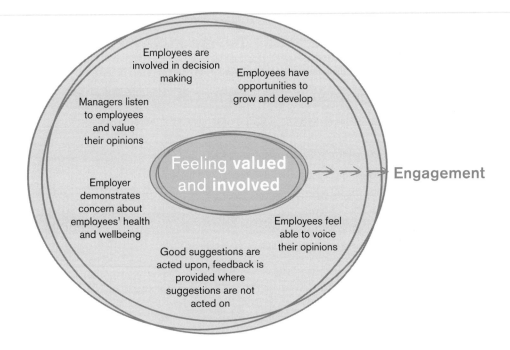

# ● MAXIMISE ENGAGEMENT AND DISCRETIONARY EFFORT

## Exploring your approach to maximise engagement and discretionary effort in your team

This questionnaire gives you a quick overview of your own style of management in relation to Engagement and Discretionary effort in your team.

Indicate which option best describes your approach in each situation, then follow the simple scoring key at the end.

| I check in with my team members: | Tick box |
|---|---|
| a. Weekly | |
| b. Daily | |
| c. When they contact me | |
| d. When I have something important to communicate to them | |

| When a member of my team has produced a high quality piece of work I: | Tick box |
|---|---|
| a. Provide recognition in the next team meeting | |
| b. Immediately give them positive feedback and/or praise | |
| c. Do nothing as I expect a high standard of work at all times | |
| d. Make a mental note to mention this situation in their next review | |

| When working with a team member to set goals and targets I: | Tick box |
|---|---|
| a. Provide some advice about the skills, competency and knowledge areas they should work on | |
| b. Encourage them to stretch their level of skill, competency and knowledge | |
| c. Encourage them to consider how other team members are doing and what they need to do to catch up | |
| d. Allow them to set goals and targets for themselves, without me interfering | |

| My attitude to raising the profile of my team members is: | Tick box |
|---|---|
| a. I am willing to tell other managers about my team members when they have produced good work | |
| b. I regularly champion my team members to other managers | |
| c. I think that profile raising is the responsibility of individual team members only | |
| d. I am willing to discuss my team members with other managers if asked | |

| When a team member comes to me with a problem I: | Tick box |
|---|---|
| a. Make an effort to listen and help in any way I can | |
| b. Consider what the employee is dealing with and try to put myself 'in their shoes' | |
| c. Ask the team member to come back to me when he/she has thought of a solution and subsequently discuss the solution | |
| d. Provide a solution that I think will work effectively | |

| I think it is most important to: | Tick box |
|---|---|
| a. Allow flexibility where possible but maintain a focus on monitoring team members | |
| b. Trust team members to deliver to deadlines and allow them to work in the way that they find most productive | |
| c. Observe team members showing commitment by coming in early and staying late to complete work on time | |
| d. Allow flexibility for special occurrences only, e.g. medical appointments | |

| When rewarding team members I think it is most important to: | Tick box |
|---|---|
| a. Ask individuals what they would like as a reward | |
| b. Consider what rewards individuals are likely to find most valuable personally | |
| c. Have a standard reward so team members can all see they are treated equally | |
| d. Ask my colleague what reward would be most appropriate for them | |

| When a key decision is being made that impacts on the team I: | Tick box |
|---|---|
| a. Send an email asking for reactions to the likely changes | |
| b. Discuss the decision and likely changes with the team at a team meeting | |
| c. Communicate the decision to the team as soon as it has been made | |
| d. Make sure the team are aware that changes are on the horizon | |

| When a team member comes to me with an idea I: | Tick box |
|---|---|
| a. Provide an evaluation of the idea and feedback about its likely success | |
| b. Listen and then coach the individual to evaluate the idea him/herself | |
| c. Ask the individual to submit the idea to me in writing | |
| d. Arrange a meeting to discuss the idea in more detail when I have more time | |

| My attitude to team members' development is: | Tick box |
|---|---|
| a. I suggest development opportunities to team members when I become aware of them | |
| b. I support team members in identifying opportunities to develop and grow | |
| c. I believe team members should take ownership for their own development and only get involved in signing off the budget for their activities | |
| d. I regularly cover development activities in performance reviews | |

## Scoring

To determine your management style, count whether you selected a, b, c or d most frequently, then read the corresponding paragraph below.

### Mostly A

You appear to have a positive approach to employee engagement and discretionary effort. Your attitude and management style are likely to be conducive to encouraging engagement within your team and eliciting discretionary effort from your team members. You may benefit from being more proactive in your approach by considering individual needs and differences at a more explicit level, trusting your team members to a greater degree and increasing the flexibility with which you enable your team to work.

### Mostly B

You are likely to have a very positive approach to employee engagement and discretionary effort. Your attitude and management style are likely to ensure that your team members remain engaged and demonstrate discretionary effort regularly. Your team members are likely to feel valued by you and involved in decision making. You could ensure that your team has consistently good levels of productivity and low turnover, by engaging with each individual on a regular basis and tailoring levels of support to their needs.

### Mostly C

You appear to prefer a management style that is quite task focused and your priorities are control, close monitoring and productivity. You may find that you focus heavily on team members' 'input' as well as their 'output'. This style is not usually as closely linked to employee engagement as more 'people focused' management styles and, as a result, you may struggle to achieve engagement from your team. It is also unlikely that they will give high levels of discretionary effort. You may benefit from relaxing your control and exploring individual differences and interests, as a first step to changing your management style. You could benefit from working to develop greater levels of trust in your team members, to allow you to shift to a predominantly 'output' focus.

### Mostly D

Although you appear to have good intentions where encouraging employee engagement is concerned, you may find that you are often too busy to properly execute your ideas. As a result, you may provide straightforward solutions that appear helpful on the surface, as opposed to exploring what different individuals really need from you. You may benefit from allocating more time to people management to enable you to focus on individual needs more closely and on a more informal basis. It is often the informal occurrences that can really make a difference to engagement and discretionary effort.

## ● NEXT STEPS

You should now be able to see the value of empowering and motivating people to achieve broader organisational goals. Consider the following suggestions for practical next steps:

### Gain feedback

Consider seeking feedback from your team/employees about how they perceive you. This may need to be confidential to encourage them to share their views. Ask them to be honest and open and review your approach as fully as possible. Check if there are any flaws or different opportunities they identify which you can alter or work on.

### Meet up with your team

You could meet with your team on an individual or group level, to discuss what more you could do for them: do they have enough of your time, do you speak with them frequently enough, could you give them more support?

Ensure you make time to get to know each of your team members individually — seek to understand what makes them tick, what they are interested in, what they think about their work. By understanding individuals, you can tailor your approach to their needs; for example, different people like to receive recognition in different ways.

### Use the exercises in this tool

To explore whether your management style is likely to encourage employee engagement and discretionary effort, do the quick and simple questionnaire provided above. Use the output from the questionnaire to start to understand the impact you have on your team/employees. Try this approach and see how it works for you.

## Look for opportunities to practise

Think about opportunities in your current work, or beyond, where you can practise engaging and motivating others to achieve aims and objectives. Think about how to do this and what the results might be.

## Write a development plan

Make 'engaging others to deliver organisational goals' a personal objective and make it a part of your own development plan. Make sure you give yourself clear objectives and actions to help you to progress and make a real improvement.

# ● FURTHER INFORMATION

If you found this tool useful then you are likely to find the following tools both insightful and relevant:

- How to engage others to deliver
- How to be assertive
- How to influence others
- How to create team identity
- How to gain buy-in and commitment
- How to maintain momentum
- How to win and manage resources.

# ● REFERENCES

1 Asch, S. (1951). Effects of group pressure upon the modification and distortion of judgement. In H. Guetzkow (ed.) **Groups, leadership and men**. Pittsburgh, PA: Carnegie Press.

2 Cialdini, R. et al (1975). Reciprocal concessions procedure for inducing compliance: The door-in-the-face technique. **Journal of Personality and Social Psychology**, 31, 206-215.

3 Sale, N. Rose, P. & Page N. (2004). **Effective Management of Global Diversity Research Panel.** Pearn Kandola.

4 The Gallup Organisation, (2004). www.gallup.com

5 Robinson, D. Perryman, S. & Hayday, S. (2004). **The Drivers of Employee Engagement**, Institute for Employment Studies.

6 Harter, J., Schmidt, F. & Hayes, T. (2002). Business unit relationship between. employee satisfaction, employee engagement and business outcomes: A metaanalysis. **Journal of Applied Psychology**, 87, 268-279.

# HOW TO IMPROVE PROCESSES

Identify processes that could benefit from improvements, as well as ways in which these improvements can be developed.

## ● ISN'T IT INTERESTING?

### Once upon a time...

Have you ever wondered why stories can be spellbinding or so powerful? We all use stories in our problem solving – we just might not know it. We use 'scripts' to help us deal with events such as a restaurant script which tells us how to behave, and what to expect, in a restaurant from our experiences. Similarly, when we read or hear stories, we are assisted in our interpretation by 'story schemas'. Schemas are bodies of knowledge that provide frameworks for understanding, for encoding new knowledge and for retrieving information. Our ability to spot and identify problems or improvements is thought to depend on how developed our schemas and scripts are.

### Spot the clue

In 1980, Gick and Holyoak[1] carried out a study into solution development where participants were presented with a problem to solve. The researchers wanted to see under what conditions people would be able to spot and spontaneously apply already existing and effective solutions to the new problem they were presented with.

They split people into three groups. Group 1 were instructed to read a story about a similar problem (in a different context) and the way in which it was solved and were given a hint that the solution to their problem might have been in the story. Group 2 were asked to read the story as well but were not given the hint. Group 3 did not read the story at all.

The results showed that most people who had been told the story and given the hint had no problem applying it to their own problem. Without this knowledge, however, very few participants were spontaneously able to spot the analogy and resolve their problem in an effective way. Most took the longer route of trying to think of several new, but incorrect, solutions.

## This tool can help

There are many situations where it isn't necessary to re-invent the wheel but rather look at what is being done or has been done already to learn from experience. This tool is about **how to improve processes** and will help you to identify processes that could benefit from improvements as well as the ways in which these improvements can be developed.

# ● CULTURE OF CONTINUOUS IMPROVEMENT

It's easy to complain when something's not working – it lets us vent our annoyance. In a corporate environment, however, serious consideration should be given to all the possible impacts of change.

All of a sudden, whatever it was you used to complain about is gone, but now you need training to deal with a new system – and change can be uncomfortable! The impact of change can be far reaching and complex – here's how to help deal with change or avoid it altogether!

Change within an organisation must be properly managed. It's easy enough to correct a single process but it's more daunting if it involves introducing complete new systems or technology – and getting people 'on side'. For more information on gaining buy-in refer to the tool 'How to gain buy-in and commitment'.

A culture of continuous change and improvement prevents an organisation from stagnating and helps it remain competitive. However, it's essential to recognise the potential problems associated with change itself.

Change, when introduced effectively, can be a seamless and easy process. However, it takes careful planning, as you're about to find out…

# ● 'IF IT AIN'T BROKE, DON'T FIX IT'

Processes – series of actions to achieve an end result – are part of our day-to-day existence, whether we're aware of them or not. Many happen without due thought even about their correctness or usefulness. We notice them only when things don't work the way we expect.

## So why do we need to improve processes?

Some businesses are more process-driven than others. Many processes work for years without needing to be changed; others need constant tinkering because of changes in technology, legislation or market conditions.

Think about processes at work. Think about one you hate because it takes too long, is difficult or fiddly.

Why is this so complicated?

Who thought this system was a good idea?

Why can't we just get this done?

It's often easy to think that something could be done differently, or that it's a complete waste of time, but try to imagine life without some of those processes you complain about.

## Consider, however, this process

Not too many years ago, receiving your salary involved taking a cheque to your bank in your lunch hour, waiting in a queue to pay it in and then waiting several days for it to clear.

Now, most of our salaries are paid straight into our accounts overnight, and we have immediate access to the money.

That's an improved process, enabled by advances in technology. You can bet, however, that when it was introduced there were those who warned it was bound to cause all manner of problems and, anyway, the old system worked well most of the time, so why the change?

Now, of course, we don't give this process a thought until, very rarely, our salary doesn't arrive in our account, and we decide it's a rotten process which someone should do something about.

## Is there really a problem?

'Continuous improvement' is currently most quality managers' 'thing'. And it's a great concept – as long as it's kept in context. It's often just as productive or wise – if a system works and people find it easy to use – to leave it alone. There's no point in changing processes wholesale just for the sake of it. In fact, it can be unnecessarily stressful and disruptive for an entire organisation and everyone in it.

Over time, processes will need revision and amendment as circumstances change but the key to smooth, easily assimilated change is to establish exactly what the problem or priority is – and fix that bit only.

On the other hand, people can be possessive about certain processes (usually the ones who thought them up in the first place or others who've got clever and cosy using them over the years!). You'll face less resistance if you make time and effort to win people over by involving them – give them a part to play and some 'ownership' of the change process itself.

### Remember, first establish:

- What is the problem?
- Who is having problems?
- Why do the problems occur?
- When do the problems occur?

### Then, before deciding on any changes, ask:

- What options are there for fixing it?
- What impact will any changes have?

## Step 2

Once you are clear about what 'importance' means to you, you are ready to prioritise tasks. List some of the tasks you've been asked to complete in the last couple of weeks and rate the importance of each on a scale of 1 to 10, where 10 is 'extremely important'.

Next, consider why they are important. We think some tasks are important just because we do them automatically – but where do they fit on your scale? Again, you might need to think again about what you think is 'important'.

Urgency: Now, rate the urgency of each task on a scale of 1 to 5, where 5 is 'deadline imminent'. (Notice that the 'Urgency' scale only goes up to 5 – because your first consideration was to rate a task's 'Importance.')

Priority: Next, add the 'Importance' and 'Urgency' scores. The tasks with the highest scores are those that you should focus on and do first.

# ● 'WE NEED TO IMPROVE THIS PROCESS'

How often do you hear that, or say it yourself? Unfortunately, when a system fails, the root cause can be difficult to identify in the crescendo of users' frustration! However, we will guide you through the problem, from identification to resolution. We will help you identify problems and win support for change from your colleagues. At the same time, we will remind you of the need for continuous improvement and, most importantly, continual review. This is no solo task – it has to involve others from the beginning because, ultimately, a process is only as good as its users!

There are four key stages in the process of continual review:

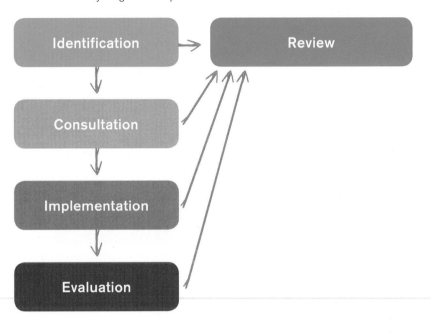

When identifying needs for change, establish whether it's about a process itself or some other factor such as staff training or a change in business direction. Here are some pointers:

- What is wrong?
- How far through the process is it?
- Is it the whole process?
- Is there a training need?
- Is the problem with the process caused by someone else further along the line?
- What is the impact of the problem?
- Who is responsible for this process?
- How widespread is the issue?

It's important to review the answers to the above questions before moving on to the consultation phase (which you might discover you don't need if it's a specific problem that can be easily put right).

**Consultation** + **Review**

If the answers given during the identification phase don't provide an obvious solution then you need a thorough consultation phase. Think about the following:

- Who has been affected by the process?
- Who would be affected by the improvement?
- How widespread has the problem been?
- Are all people following the process correctly?
- What do people feel the solution is?
- Is the solution a 'simple fix' or does it involve total renewal?

Make a point of consulting people who use the process – not just a small group of managers:

1. It's reasonable that people who use the process are qualified to offer ideas.
2. They will feel included in the process which then makes it easier to introduce changes.

If this phase has been conducted properly then you should have a clear understanding of the problem plus some ideas for correcting it. This is the stage where you'll be able to tell whether a bit of tweaking is all that's needed, or a whole new process.

**Implementation** + **Review**

The review from the Consultation Phase should have given you enough information to know what to do and the Implementation Phase assists in the doing of it! It's vital, however to review continually throughout the Implementation Phase, because this is the time to check things are working or amend as necessary.

So, when planning how to put the changes in place:

- Ensure that the person who knows most about the process is given the authority and time to change things.
- Decide the best course of action and investigate how to implement it.
- Get approval for the changes from senior stakeholders to help you convince others of the need for change.
- Communicate that changes are to take place to all concerned in good time and arrange training where necessary.
- The process should be documented, kept up to date and easily accessible.
- Monitor cost implications.

**Evaluation**

From the moment you consider changing a process, evaluate all information and facts each step of the way – otherwise, problems could multiply before you complete!

Post-implementation evaluation should be done after the process has been given time to fully bed in – remember, processes that run like clockwork will have been honed and perfected over time.

# ● HELPFUL HINTS

| Identification | Key points for review | Consultation | Key points for review |
|---|---|---|---|
| What is wrong? | | Who has been affected by the process? | Was the problem brought to your attention or did you notice it? |
| How far through the process is it? | | Who would be affected by the improvement? | An issue at the beginning impacts those further along the process. |
| Is it the whole process? | | How widespread has the problem been? | How many complaints have you had? |
| Is there a training need? | | Are all people following the process correctly? | Informal chats can highlight information that might not come out as part of a focus group session (people do not want to look foolish in front of their peers). |
| Is the problem with the process caused by someone else further along the line? | | What do people feel the solution is? | Were any suggestions helpful? |
| What is the impact of the problem? | | Is the solution a simple fix or does it involve a complete reappraisal of the process? | Fingers crossed for a simple fix. |
| Who is responsible for this process? | | Does this require a completely new process or just an improvement? | What would be needed to justify a completely new process? |
| How widespread is the issue? | | | |
| Is this a process issue or is it a training issue? | | | |

| Implementation | Key points for review |
|---|---|
| Ensure that the person with the most comprehensive knowledge of the process has the decision making power and the time to change things. | Is the key person able to do this – are there time constraints? How much of a priority is it? |
| Decide the best course of action and investigate how to implement it. | This should come out from the consultation phase, as should the identification of the key person for the process. An action plan/timetable would need to be prepared for any significant changes – did this happen? |

| Implementation | Key points for review |
|---|---|
| Get approval for the changes from the top level; this makes it easier to enforce throughout the organisation. | Once plan is prepared, get it in front of senior management team for approval, even if you do not officially need it. It will make life easier further down the organisation – did this happen? |
| Successful process change and improvement is driven by training, so make sure time is allowed for communicating the changes and arrange training where necessary. | Has a training plan been put together and has it worked properly? Was the improvement communicated around the organisation (include explanation of why change is happening as it might not have affected some people)? |
| Documentation of the process needs to be created/amended and needs to be kept up to date where people can easily access it. | This should be done as a matter of course, but is it? |
| Is there a cost implication for this process? | Not all improvements involve costs, but if this does, who holds the budget? Your work to date should have enough evidence to justify any costs. |

| Evaluation |
|---|
| This is post-implementation evaluation. Depending on the size of the process change, you need to determine timeframes for evaluation; it could be a week, a month or three months after the improvement is introduced. It should not be left any longer than three months. Any problems with the process would be identified within that timeframe and if further improvements are needed, it is easier to introduce them before everyone is too entrenched in the new system. |

You have already reviewed along the way, so this evaluation is overall:

- Did the process improve?
- Was the training successful?
- Have any further problems come to light?

## ● NEXT STEPS

When an organisation is accustomed to a culture of continuous improvement, changes are introduced more easily and people feel able to flag problems as they occur – and before they escalate.

> Are you thinking about a particular process at work which hasn't changed or been thought about for years? Notwithstanding our advice that there's little point in change for change's sake, it's as well to carry out an evaluation as we've described here – and perhaps make a few small improvements at most – rather than allow disaster to creep up while your back's turned!

Also, never forget the importance of the human element to change. In a study by van Dam et al.[2] employees were surveyed for their resistance to organisational change. The three factors that contributed most strongly to their relationship to change were information, participation and trust in management. So when implementing change, you may well want to try to keep people informed and involved as much as possible in order to get the buy-in you need from your co-workers to make meaningful change happen.

# ● FURTHER INFORMATION

If you found this tool useful then you are likely to find the following tools both insightful and relevant:

- How to gain buy-in and commitment
- How to be innovative
- How to think about problems laterally
- How to make complex ideas simple, clear and concise.

# ● REFERENCES

1  Gick, M. & Holyoak, K. (1980). Analogical problem solving. **Cognitive Psychology,** 12, 306-355.

2  Furst, S. A., & Cable, D. M. (2008). Employee resistance to organizational change: Managerial influence tactics and leader-member exchange. **Journal of Applied Psychology,** 93(2), 453.

# HOW TO BE CONFIDENT IN MAKING JUDGEMENT CALLS

Discover your decision making styles and gain an insight into how others make decisions.

## ● ISN'T IT INTERESTING?

Do you see the spiral in the picture?....

### Things are not always as they appear

It may appear at first glance that there is a spiral in the centre of this image, but in fact, there is a series of perfectly round circles. This is known as a 'Fraser Illusion', first identified by Sir James Fraser in 1908.[1] This is one of many 'optical illusions' found in psychology where your vision defies the logic of your brain.

### Everyday illusions

Our vision works at a sub-conscious level; the visual cortex at the back of our brain interprets cellular input from our optic nerve automatically,[2] explaining how you will still see a spiral now even though you know one does not exist.

Illusions like this work because the context around the stimuli (the circles in this instance) is distracting. Our brain is constantly processing masses of information, and not just necessarily what you're concentrating on, which can lead to mental errors.

### This tool can help

Similar to this illusion, in our working day we are bombarded with lots of distractions and we are required to make decisions all the time. Some decisions are small and trivial whilst others are grand and highly important. By taking a step back and looking at things rationally and objectively it becomes easier to make reasoned judgement that you can be confident with.

This tool is all about **how to be confident in making judgement calls** and helps you to discover your decision making styles as well as providing you with insight into how others make decisions too. Knowing your decision making styles and when to apply them can increase your confidence in the judgements that you make.

# ● DECISION MAKING STYLES

If you are confident about your decisions in the past, you are likely to believe that you made a good decision and you were competent at the time you made it. This feeling of confidence that you have made the right decision is influenced by the way in which you reached it. For example, you may feel more confident that you have made the right decision if you have written down all of the possible solutions and made a list of pros and cons for each one before deciding on the best course of action.

Everyone has their own preferred decision making style that enables them to make judgement calls and important decisions. Your preferred decision making style can be influenced by many things, including preparation of information and knowledge of the topic area. Indeed, it is often the case that people feel more confident when they know the subject area or have a strategy for making the judgement call. However, in order to explore your confidence in making judgement calls you need to go a step further and consider your personality and your preferences. There are no right or wrong personality types, and different decision making styles will work better or worse in different situations. An awareness of your characteristic preferences or style of making decisions can give you insight into other perspectives you might not have considered. Raising your awareness of other perspectives that may have otherwise gone unnoticed will give you the opportunity to consider more options or approach decision making in another way. This will provide you with a more thorough approach and help you to feel more confident that you have made the right choice.

When making decisions, considering other options, factoring in what others might feel or think about the decision can help give you confidence in your judgements. There will always be people with different personalities to yourself and those who have decision making styles different from yours, but you can build confidence in your decisions and judgements if you know that you have considered all the angles.

Understanding your personality profile will help you recognise how you prefer to make decisions. From this you can see where your strengths are and where you need to consider other options. For example, if you have a low score on Agreeableness you are likely to be more task focused than people focused.

This is great in terms of getting a task completed but you may need to think about how your decisions will affect other people around you.

It is generally accepted amongst researchers that there are five broad domains that describe different aspects of personality.[3] A review by McRae & Costa of the 5-factor personality model describes high scorers in these factors as follows:

- **Extraversion** – A strong desire to be involved with others socially, participation in team/group events, and ability to outwardly display these feelings.

- **Openness to Experience** – Interest in wide range of events such as travel, cusine, etc. A need for novelty, change and variety.

- **Conscientiousness** – A strong sense of purpose, a striving and accomplishment based internal drive, as well as a tendency to plan for the long-term rather than short-term reward.

- **Agreeableness** – A forgiving and generous nature, belief in cooperation with others and a desire to avoid inter-personal conflict.

- **Neuroticism** – A worried nature, including low self-esteem, self-doubt and perfectionist and pessimistic approaches to one's own actions.

As individuals, our personalities are made up of an infinite combination of these scales. However, it can be useful to look at where we fall on each scale, how that might impact on our decision making style and which areas we might not characteristically consider.

The 'Big 5' personality factors have been shown over many years of research to be directly relevant to the workplace. A recent meta-study[4] examining the results of many studies into these personality factors found positive relationships between factors such as conscientousness and openness to experience and work performance and job satisfaction.

# ● EFFECTIVELY MAKING JUDGEMENT CALLS

The information above provided an overview of how awareness of your personality can help you to further develop your decision making style and therefore feel more confident in the decisions you make. This exercise will help you to identify your personality profile, information you might often fail to consider ('blind spots') and show you how you can use a broader approach for decision making in future. Use the worksheet on page 105 to complete this exercise.

## Step one

Using the personality questions below, identify which aspect of each personality trait you identify with most.

## Step two

Read through the information on decision making style to make your choices. If there are any scales that you feel don't fully reflect your style, that's OK – make a note of them on the worksheet (on page 105).

## Personality questions

For each scale below, choose which of the 2 descriptions is most like you:

### 1. Extraversion

Are you more

**a)** Outgoing, gregarious, needing lots of social interaction and stimulation?

**OR**

**b)** Quiet, reflective, with a preference for spending more time on your own?

**Extraversion decision making style**

a) You may prefer a decision making style that gets ideas, information and energy from other people. You may instinctively involve stakeholders in the decision making to solicit opinion and get others on board. You will feel confident with your decision because you have gathered lots of opinions. This may mean, however, that you can tend to rely on others to help you in making decisions and you may find it more difficult to be confident in making decisions by yourself.

b) You may prefer a decision making style that allows you to reflect on the information you have, on your own. When you need to involve others you are likely to do so with one other or a small group. The benefit of this can be diverse information and candid opinions. You may, however, risk not consulting with others and therefore missing important information with which to make your decision.

## 2. Openness to experience

Are you more

a) interested in new experiences, ways of doing things, and ideas?

OR

b) prefer more established ways of doing things – 'hands on', more practical?

### Openness decision making style

If you answered (a) you may have a preference for a decision making style that centres on creativity. This is where you can develop creative solutions to a problem. It is a freewheeling way of thinking, in which there is little criticism of ideas. A whole range of creativity tools can help you here. You may risk being overly focused on new ideas and ways of doing things rather than making the decision itself and you may delay this stage.

If you answered (b) your preferred decision making style may be to focus on the data available. You look at the information you have, and see what you can learn from it. You look for gaps in your knowledge, and either try to fill them or take account of them. This is where you analyse past trends, and try to extrapolate from historical data. You could benefit from ensuring that you take yourself away from the data at times to consider new ways of doing things.

## 3. Conscientiousness

Which is more like you

a) Organised, conscientious, compliant and someone who pays attention to the details?

OR

b) Chaotic, unplanned, spontaneous – a risk taker?

### Decision making style

If you answered a) you are likely to have a planned decision making style when making important or complicated decisions. In other words, you gather information and apply a systematic and deliberate approach that is a balance between logical reasoning and intuition. A planned approach takes time and energy but is worthwhile when you have to make important decisions. You will also be more confident with your decision if you know you have done your homework and it feels right intuitively. You run the risk of needing all of the information to make a decision and you may not be overly comfortable with ambiguity.

If you answered (b) you may have a more spontaneous style of decision making – gathering some information but feeling comfortable and ready to act even when and as soon as you have difficult information. You will be unafraid of taking risks, having to change strategies at short notice, or amending your decisions in light of new information. You need to ensure that you consider all of the evidence that you have, or need, in order to make the most informed decision.

## 4. Agreeableness

Are you

a) Focused on people, maintaining harmonious relationships, concerned with the emotional needs of others?

OR

b) Focused on the task, what needs to be done, speak your mind?

### Decision making style

If you answered (a) you may make your decisions using 'gut reaction' and emotion. You may also try to think how other people will react emotionally. You will try to understand others' reactions to your decision, and take this into account when making a judgement call. You may need to ensure that you focus on the logic and rationale behind the decision, especially when decisions involve more analytical types.

If you answered (b) you may make your decision by focusing on the task that needs to be completed, the process that needs to be followed and the deliverable outcomes. You are unlikely to be overly focused on the feelings or emotions of the individuals involved if they are likely to impede progress. You run the risk of not considering other people's feelings when making decisions and you should try to factor this into your decision making.

### 5. Neuroticism

Are you more

a) Calm, consistent under pressure, confident in own opinions?

**OR**

b) Anxious, emotionally expressive, reflective, somewhat self critical?

### Decision making style

If you answered (a) your decision making style indicates that you are likely to think positively. It is this optimistic viewpoint that helps you to see all the benefits of the decision and the value in it. It can help you to keep going when everything looks gloomy or difficult. You need to ensure that you are being realistic and not overly optimistic as well as considering the potential risks and threats.

If you answered (b) your decision making style is likely to identify all of the bad points of the decision. Look at it cautiously and defensively. Try to see why it might not work. This is important because it highlights the weak points in a plan. It allows you to eliminate them, alter them, or prepare contingency plans to counter them. It helps to make your plans 'tougher' and more resilient. It can also help you to spot fatal flaws and risks before you embark on a course of action. You need to make sure that you are also considering the potential opportunities and benefits as you may overlook these in your approach.

## Step three

Now look at the information on the decision making styles that DO NOT match with your personality responses – these are where you may have decision making 'blind spots'. In the table on the next page, complete the first column 'Potential decision making blind spot' by noting the styles that you feel don't represent your normal approach to decision making. Do this for each of the five decision making styles described above.

## Step four

When next making a judgement call or important decision – start by following your usual decision making process. However, before you make your final decision, look through your table and consider the decision and its outcome from the 'blind spots' or perspectives you would not normally consider. in the table, make a note of what you could do, or what you could consider, from each perspective and write them in the columns marked 'Decision 1', 'Decision 2' and 'Decision 3'.

Add this information into your decision making process. This will allow you to have increased confidence in your final decision.

Decision 1

| | Potential decision making blind spot | The decision |
|---|---|---|
| Extraversion | | |
| Openness to experience | | |
| Conscientiousness | | |
| Agreeableness | | |
| Neuroticism | | |

Decision 2

| | Potential decision making blind spot | The decision |
|---|---|---|
| Extraversion | | |
| Openness to experience | | |
| Conscientiousness | | |
| Agreeableness | | |
| Neuroticism | | |

Decision 3

| | Potential decision making blind spot | The decision |
|---|---|---|
| Extraversion | | |
| Openness to experience | | |
| Conscientiousness | | |
| Agreeableness | | |
| Neuroticism | | |

## Share your information

Share this information with a mentor, or someone who knows your management and working style. Discuss the areas that need development, and the dynamics of the situation you found yourself in. Ask them for feedback, for example to help shed light on a blind spot. This will also help you to understand your decision making style in more depth, e.g. what works well, what doesn't and how your style impacts on others.

## ● NEXT STEPS

The exercise above is designed to help you discover your preferences in making judgement calls. Increasing your level of self-awareness should help you to understand how you can be most effective in getting the decisions right. This, in turn, serves to increase confidence in making judgement calls. There are a number of actions that you could do next:

### Look for opportunities to practise

Think about judgements calls coming up that you feel very confident with and those you feel less confident with. Start by tackling those that you feel more at ease with to build your confidence before moving on to the more challenging situations.

### Reflect on past experiences

Think about a time when you made a judgement call but the 'wheels fell off'. Think about your decision making style, using the questionnaire on the previous page, and try to identify what the issues were, and what style you are.

### Write a development plan

Prepare a development plan for building your confidence, highlighting any 'blind spots' (from the table above) that need development. Then set in place a future date for evaluation when you can re-visit the judgement calls you have made in the workplace and see what the difference has been in your approach since the first meeting.

## ● FURTHER INFORMATION

If you found this tool useful then you are likely to find the following tools both insightful and relevant:

- How to be assertive
- How to make timely decisions
- How to make reasoned judgements
- How to balance risk with potential benefits
- How to take responsibility
- How to take control
- How to know when and how to take risks
- How to use optimism to achieve.

## ● REFERENCES

1 Fraser, J. (1908). A new visual illusion of direction. British Journal of Psychology, 2, 307–320.

2 Snowden, R., Thompson, P., & Troscianko, T. (2012). Basic Vision: an introduction to visual perception. OUP Oxford.

3 McCrae, R. R., & Costa Jr, P. T. (1999). A five-factor theory of personality. Handbook of personality: Theory and research, 2, 139-153.

4 Barrick, M. R., & Mount, M. K. (2006). The big five personality dimensions and job performance: a meta-analysis. Personnel psychology, 44(1), 1-26.

# CHALLENGING

# HOW TO CHALLENGE OTHERS EFFECTIVELY

Develop an understanding of how to challenge others, and discover what is stopping you from doing this.

## ● ISN'T IT INTERESTING?

The White Flag as a classic image of surrender is thought to originate from the Eastern Han dynasty in what is now China (AD 25–220).[1] It signifies an unarmed negotiator, intention to surrender or a desire to communicate.

### Getting others on board

There are many different ways to challenge people effectively. One classic example where leaders made disastrous mistakes by not challenging one another happened in 1961 with John F Kennedy's failed invasion of Cuba. This phenomenon is known as 'Groupthink' and occurs when team members value harmony and consensus over full appraisal of the situation. It occurs most often when team members are similar, have close relationships, lack self-confidence and have a strong leader who takes sides. This effect has been seen in historical contexts, even as far back as the 'Sanhedrin' in ancient Israel[2] where the legislative body designed several regulations described in ancient holy texts which show the use of coping strategies to prevent incidents of groupthink.

### The Bay of Pigs

Kennedy consulted with his top advisors regarding a CIA and military plan to use Cuban exiles to overthrow Fidel Castro. They decided on a covert invasion. However, Castro was alerted to the threat, leading to the invaders being vastly outnumbered and lacking air support, ammunition and an escape route. This resulted in 1,200 US soldiers surrendering, and the death of others.

The following investigation found that Kennedy's advisors did not challenge bad ideas in case this upset group cohesion. For instance, the Presidential advisor presented serious objections to the invasion in a memorandum to the president, but did not express these at team meetings.

Individuals not raising their concerns and not challenging others' decisions or views led to poor decision making in this case. The group thought they could not be defeated, the issues and problems were rationalised away and they stereotyped the opposition as weaker than them. As a consequence of the Bay of Pigs disaster, President Kennedy changed the decision making process to ensure this would encourage debate – this alone prevented potential future catastrophes.

## This tool can help

It is not always easy to challenge others, especially when you do not know what the reaction will be or you are worried about the predicted reaction. This tool is about **How to challenge others effectively** and will help you to develop an understanding of how to challenge well, and discovering what is stopping you from doing this. You can begin to develop knowledge and experience of different techniques that you can use to challenge others, including body language.

## ● HOW TO CHALLENGE OTHERS EFFECTIVELY

Any functioning relationship, whether at work or elsewhere, benefits when the parties are able to challenge each other in ways that increase understanding, or allow mutually acceptable decision making and resolution of disagreements.

Great theory. The truth is that many of us avoid challenging anyone or anything, because we're worried either about making fools of ourselves, or about the reaction we might get. Even so, most of us would agree that we each have a right to make known our views and feelings about things. It's a tricky one – not wanting to 'rock the boat', exactly, but not minding if the other person fell overboard, either…

We'll show you how to challenge constructively in a variety of circumstances, so, first, here's a model of different attitudes, or kinds of challenge (we call these 'stances') Our 'stance' depends on what we think and how we feel. That is, our mindset and level of aggression – the appropriateness of which depends on the situation.

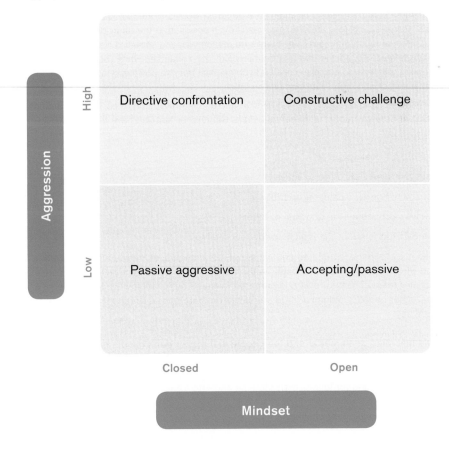

A Passive Aggressive stance is rarely effective, because it allows neither open discussion nor explanation. The three other stances in the model, however, are effective in different circumstances.

For example, where there is a need to concede one's interests in light of another's, or when the issue is of low importance to you but high importance to another, then an Accepting stance is the most constructive (if you fight the point as a matter of principle, whether you care about the outcome or not, then you'll get a reputation for being a pain in the neck in no time, and diminish your effectiveness on other occasions, when something really does matter to you).

Or, when the issue is of extreme importance and not negotiable (matters of health and safety, risk or harassment, for example) then a Directive Confrontation stance is reasonable. In most other situations where you need to be assertive, a Constructive Challenge stance is appropriate, because you come across as wishing to communicate your views and feelings, yet open minded and receptive.

## What's stopping you?

If we know we should challenge something or someone, why do we find it so difficult?

- We worry about the other person's reaction and our ability to manage it.
- We're unsure of our right to challenge someone.
- We're worried about what people will think, or that we will not be liked if we challenge someone.

Then, thinking about these possibilities makes us even more anxious and less inclined to question anything we disagree with or that affects us adversely. Instead, try to remember the following:

- Our assumptions about another's reactions are generally overestimated, or just wrong. Often, whatever's worrying us is less important or hasn't even occurred to the other person and, if you approach a situation diplomatically, there's no reason why you shouldn't be listened to. If someone does react negatively, then just remain calm and composed while you clarify whatever point you wish to make – you'll find you can still reach a positive outcome, even if it takes a little longer and more than one conversation.
- Often, for reasons of upbringing, cultural background and interpretation of social expectations we question or deny even our fundamental beliefs. Remember that you have the right to:[2]
  - Make mistakes
  - Say 'no' without feeling guilty
  - Maintain your own view or perspective
  - Protest against unfair treatment or criticism
  - Not always worry about the goodwill of others
  - Be your own judge about the legitimacy of your feelings.
- As long as our challenge is justified and we adopt a reasonable, moderate attitude, there is no reason why people should think badly of us. In fact, the opposite is more likely, because people usually respect someone who is prepared to 'stand up for their views'. Also, we forget that other people's opinions of us are based on more than a single incident. As your mum might say:

'The people that mind don't matter and the people that matter don't mind!'

- Remember, it might take a bit of courage to challenge someone, but saying nothing often makes things worse and for longer than the time and effort needed to speak up.

Take the plunge and make that challenge!

# ● SIMPLE TECHNIQUES FOR CONSTRUCTIVE CHALLENGE

## Own your feelings

Instead of making assumptions and talking about what someone else thinks or intends (which you may never fully appreciate), speak from your own perspective and describe your own feelings. This allows the other person to recognise how his or her behaviour is interpreted by you and, possibly, others. For example, instead of: **'You upset me when you don't listen'** try **'when you talk over me, it makes me think you're not listening and I feel upset'**. The first explanation 'blames' whereas the second 'explains'.

## Describe the behaviour, not the person

If someone thinks you're criticising them as a person, they're likely to react negatively. Instead, describe the specific behaviour you're challenging because this is something that can be modified or changed. Instead of: **'You are aggressive and rude'** try **'when you point at people and tell them they are wrong, it comes across as aggressive and could be perceived as rude'**. This is about recognising that there can be a difference between someone's intention, and how others interpret their behaviour.

## Be specific

Decide exactly what it is you want or feel and communicate it clearly and briefly. That doesn't mean being perfunctory and rude – just don't chew on it and make it even more of an issue.

## Repeat important messages

Repeat your clear, specific statement until the other person has heard and responded. This is particularly useful if you're feeling nervous, or dealing with someone who is manipulative or aggressive. It can also avoid getting tangled up in arguments and justifications.

## Acknowledge and field responses

To show that you've heard what someone has said to you, it's important to acknowledge it. All you need to do is repeat it without making any comment, then repeat your own statement, e.g. **'I understand that it will mean changing the holiday rotas because I want to take my holiday in July this year.'**

## Find a workable compromise

When there is a genuine conflict of interest, there doesn't have to be a 'winner' and a 'loser'. If you treat each other as equal and consider each other's needs, you should both get enough of whatever it is you want, to feel able to give something back without feeling resentful!

## Self disclose

Sometimes we might want and intend to be assertive, but get 'hijacked' by our emotions. Just say how you feel, simply and in a clear, direct way (we call this 'self-disclosure').

## Use negative assertion

This is a useful way to deal with criticism. Usually, we deny whatever it is and become defensive or shirty! We can diffuse negativity for both parties, however, by simply acknowledging the criticism and offering to adapt our behaviour in a given situation: **'Yes, I am impulsive. That's my natural way, will it cause us any problems?'**

## Use negative enquiry

Asking a diplomatically worded question avoids sounding overtly critical ('negative assertion'), by making us appear willing to acknowledge contributing to a problem, if appropriate. For example: **'You've been a bit distant lately, have I done something to upset you?'**

## Check your body language

Assertive body language reinforces our message, non-assertive body language confuses it. Your body language needs to be consistent with your message. However, by 'assertive' we don't mean standing over someone with your hands on your hips, or poking a finger at them! We're talking about maintaining eye contact and a relaxed or customary facial expression.

## Posture and distance

Make sure you're neither standing over the person nor appearing to distance yourself from them. If they are sitting or standing, do the same.

## Mouth

If we're nervous we can get tense and clench our jaw or tighten our mouths. Consciously relax your face, if you can — but don't smile to ingratiate yourself or mitigate what you're saying, because that, again, sends mixed messages and confuses the other person.

## Voice

Try not to mumble, as if you're unconvinced about what you're saying — or talk more loudly than normal, as though discouraging any response. If you think you're doing either, stop and breathe for a moment or two. In fact, pausing every so often is another effective way to reinforce what you're saying, anyway!

## Gestures

Try not to fiddle with your hands, your nose or twiddle your hair — you'll look nervous and unsure of yourself. On the other hand, striding about, waving your arms or pointing will look aggressive (if not a bit silly). Shrugging your shoulders may suggest the situation is beyond you, or you don't care anyway!

## Breathe!

Taking deep breaths really does help to calm nervousness. Prepare yourself before an assertive encounter by taking some slow, deep breaths.

### Refusing requests

This is often difficult, so while you're weighing things up, consider the following:

- Your 'gut' feeling usually tells you whether you want to agree to or refuse a request.
- If you're not sure, ask for more details so you know what you're really committing yourself to.
- Don't be afraid to say 'No' rather than deferring to a higher authority.
- Make it clear you're refusing the request, not the person, the role, the job or the friendship.
- If you feel guilty when you say 'No' to something you don't want to do, think of it as saying 'Yes' to yourself — your self worth.
- Saying 'No', and surviving the guilt, gets easier — just keep practising!

# ● PREPARING TO CHALLENGE EFFECTIVELY

Thinking through your approach can help reduce nervousness about challenging someone, and give you a different perspective – both on the issue and the appropriateness of your reaction. Try not to brood or seethe about it though, – just calmly clarify the 'what' and 'why' of it. To help you, we've designed a checklist for you to keep and use whenever the need arises:

| Challenge Effectively | Tick |
|---|---|
| Why do you need to challenge this person? | |
| What specifically do you want? | |
| What are your feelings on the issue? | |
| How is it affecting you? | |
| What reaction do you expect from the other person/other people? | |
| Why do you think they will react like this? What would their reason be? | |
| What positive things do they know about you/feel towards you? | |
| What might be a good compromise? | |
| What are the benefits of avoiding the confrontation? | |
| What are the drawbacks? | |
| What are the potential drawbacks of making the challenge? | |
| What are the benefits? | |

Finally, how will you begin the conversation? Make sure you're straightforward, non-accusatory and honest. For example: 'Could we make some time to talk about something that's really bothering me? I'm really concerned about our working relationship.'

## Summary

Often, preparation is the key to success. Effective, successful challenging improves rather than worsens situations, and it's a skill that needs practise. Keeping going, even if it doesn't work out perfectly the first time, learn what you need to from the experience, and don't resign yourself to being a pushover!

# ● FURTHER INFORMATION

If you found this tool useful then you are likely to find the following tools both insightful and relevant:

- How to be assertive
- How to influence others
- How to communicate effectively
- How to manage your impact
- How to support and challenge in tandem
- How to give feedback
- How to take control.

# ● REFERENCES

1   http://www.worldflags101.com/other-flags/white-flag.aspx

2   Schnall, E., & Greenberg, M. J. (2012). Groupthink and the Sanhedrin: An analysis of the ancient court of Israel through the lens of modern social psychology. **Journal of Management History**, 18(3), 285-294.

3   Davis, M. et al. (2000). **The Stress and Relaxation Workbook**, New Harbinger, CA.

# HOW TO BALANCE RISK WITH POTENTIAL BENEFITS

Understand the psychology of decision making, how to balance risks with benefits and how to be more effective in your work as a result.

## ● ISN'T IT INTERESTING?

Compete or collaborate?

### Balancing risk

There are some of us who are born competitors, whilst others are all about cooperation and consensus; most of us are somewhere in between. This is related to our innate sense of whether to run away or to stay and work through the situation – the fight or flight response.[1] Although we can be naturally competitive or collaborative, we often adapt our approach through our experience. A well known piece of psychological research conducted in the 1960s[2] aimed to show how experience enables us to learn to respond differently to situations.

### The prisoner's dilemma

Consider this issue: Detectives interview two prisoners separately and afterwards decide that there is only adequate evidence to convict them for a lesser offence. The police separately offer these individuals the opportunity to confess. However, if one confesses and the other does not then the confessor will have immunity and the evidence will be used to convict the other individual on the more serious offence. If both confess, both get the lighter sentence, and if neither confesses then the sentence will be very light.

The prisoner's dilemma creates a matrix. Mutual silence is the best shared outcome for the prisoners, yet a degree of suspicion and lack of trust can often lead to a confession from both parties. This study has been duplicated with hundreds of prisoners and it seems that people are torn between competing with one another and cooperating, as their fate rests on both people's choices.

Prisoner A

| | Confesses | | Does not confess | |
|---|---|---|---|---|
| Confesses | 3 years | 3 years | 0 years | 6 years |
| Does not confess | 6 years | 0 years | 6 months | 6 months |

Prisoner B

## This tool can help

Most of us are hopefully not required to balance risks and benefits as they did in the above exercise. However, it does indicate that this is a complex process and that there are many considerations we have to take into account when balancing risks and benefits for a desired outcome. This tool is about **how to balance risk with potential benefits** and will help you to understand this and be more effective as a result.

# ● RATIONALITY OF DECISION MAKING

Decision making is the process of selection from different options. It's about reasoning, even though the selection made can sometimes seem anything but 'reasonable' to an onlooker! This is because our reasoning can be rational or irrational, based on explicit or implicit assumptions — and even on beliefs for which we have no evidence.

## How a rational decision is made

When making a rational decision, we come to our judgement on a purely factual basis. In order to do this we must follow a logical formula, such as this one:[3]

Utility = (probability x value) of all individual factors

So, if the utility of an action is its impact, this is determined by a sum of factors possibly resulting from the action. What determines the utility is the value of the effect(s) which is then multiplied by the probability of the result occurring.

This is a purely rational decision making model, and as this tool will explain, is generally altered by our own assumptions and biases.

Decision making is what we call a 'psychological construct'. All this means is that something has happened of which there's no external indication. However, because it will noticeably affect subsequent behaviour, we understand or deduce that a decision has been made or has 'happened'.

Decision making is fundamental to learning — it is a process of sifting and making sense of information, during which we typically progress through a 4-stage cycle:

1. Immediate or concrete experiences i.e. actions or behaviours
2. Observations and reflections i.e. thoughts and ideas
3. Formulation of abstract concepts i.e. strategies and theories
4. Active testing of these new concepts[4] i.e. activities

Decision making is important at each stage, but particularly to observation and reflection (Stage 2). Once a decision is made, it becomes the new concept that we can test at Stage 4, which in turn provides us with a new experience — and so the cycle begins again and continues…

## 'Groupthink'

This is a common development amongst people who co-exist or work together regularly. It's the adoption by the majority, of a more dominant minority's attitudes and opinions. It can stifle creativity and — catastrophically, sometimes — personal responsibility (it's often blamed for the Challenger shuttle disaster[5]). This is a key indication of how bias can affect decision making, and how even a few strong dissenting voices can direct the decisions of a majority into dangerous grounds.

However, awareness of bias such as groupthink can lead to effective strategies to combat bias, and these strategies were put into motion in the wake of the Challenger disaster to good effect.

For more information on preventing groupthink, there are relevant sections in the tool 'How to challenge others effectively'.

Developing your decision making skills will help you and your team make sure the decisions you make are balanced, in terms of risk and benefit.

## ● BIASES IN DECISION MAKING

Bias means 'tendency' or 'preference'. We can be aware of our own biases, or not – they can be subconscious. This means our decision making can be influenced by factors which may have no bearing on the matter we're dealing with.

Here are some examples of biases many of us hold, knowingly or unknowingly:

| Bias | Definition |
| --- | --- |
| Selective bias | This is a tendency to focus or gather facts which support what we anticipate, or hope for. We therefore disregard other facts which may support alternative conclusions. |
| Discontinuation of evidence searching | A tendency to accept the first alternative that looks as if it might work – rather than checking that others might not be as good or better. |
| Unwillingness to change | We may develop patterns of behaviour according to our experiences, and continue them even in different or unrelated circumstances. In this way, we'd do something a certain way without considering whether it's the best option. |
| Rebelliousness | A tendency to do other than what is wanted, expected or demanded by others – especially those perceived to be in a position of authority. |
| Experienced-based limitations | An unwillingness or inability to look beyond our own experiences. This can result as much from fear of trying something new, as from arrogance. |
| Selective perception | Actively filtering information we personally consider irrelevant or insignificant to a particular decision. |
| Optimism | Deliberately disregarding potential problems, which distorts our thinking as much as pessimism! |
| Choice/supportive bias | We 're-script' our memory of available options and the reasons for our decision, to reassure ourselves (and others) that it's 'better' or more desirable than it may originally have seemed! |
| Recency effect | Attention is given to new or recent facts and data rather than existing or previous information, which can be ignored or forgotten. |
| Primacy effect | This is the opposite of the 'Recency effect' – original information is adhered to and new facts or data ignored. |
| Repetition bias | A tendency to unquestioning belief in what we're told, or in what we're told by most of those around us. |
| Anchoring or adjustment | Decisions based on previous information subsequently influence our approach to new or fresh information. |
| Peer pressure or groupthink | Conforming to the opinions of our peers, or people important to us at a particular time. |

| Bias | Definition |
|------|-----------|
| Source credibility bias | Refusal to accept or acknowledge information which contradicts our bias against, say, a person or a group – or even a group to which a particular person belongs. We can also be influenced to this kind of bias by someone we like or admire. |
| Irregularities | Not using the same criteria when making decisions in similar situations. |
| Attributions | Attributing our own success to our abilities and talents – but our failures to chance or factors beyond our control. Conversely, those of us with this kind of bias turn it around where others are concerned, assuming their successes are 'flukes' and their failures an inevitable result of their own mistakes or lack of ability! |
| Self Fulfilling Prophecy | This is where we conform to others' expectations of us but often for quite different reasons than theirs. |
| Illusion of control | Overestimating our control of events. This is often a result of wishing to minimise potential problems arising from decisions we've made. |
| Generalisations | We can do this in order to simplify a complex situation or event; the trouble is, we then make inappropriate, simplistic decisions about complex matters. |
| Causal | Making assumptions which are not based on facts. Just because someone leaves the room when you walk in doesn't mean they left because you came in – they may simply have finished what they were doing! |

## ● IDENTIFY YOUR BIASES IN DECISION MAKING

Using the table from the previous two pages, make a note of what you think are five biases that you experience. Be honest – consider situations at work where you've made decisions, and think back to how you reached them.

Top five biases

1

2

3

4

5

Now, take the two strongest biases and note down any ways in which you've tried to overcome or circumvent them. Try thinking of other strategies you might use in future, as well.

Use the model overpage to capture your thoughts.

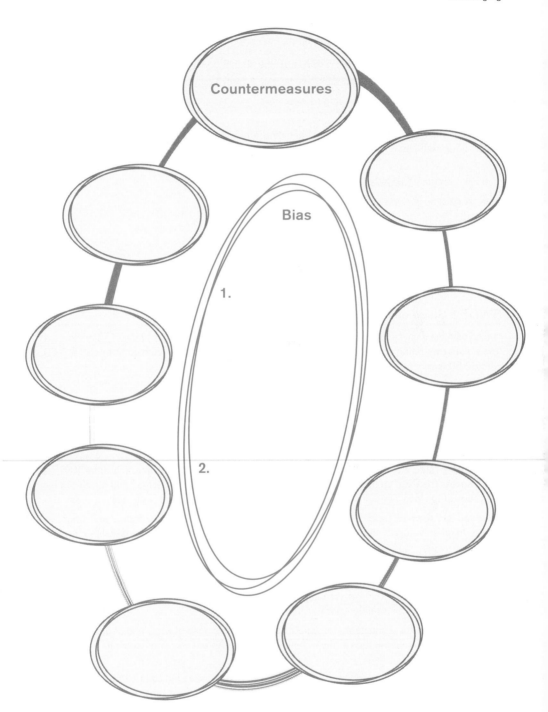

## ● BALANCING RISK EXERCISE

This will help you decide whether the risks of a particular course of action outweigh the benefits. First, carry out a SWOT analysis[6] of the situation (another acronym, this time for Strengths, Weaknesses, Opportunities and Threats):

- **Strengths** – what are the strengths that will assist you?
- **Weaknesses** – which weaknesses of your own might hinder you?
- **Opportunities** – what opportunities will result from it?
- **Threats** – what might threaten its success?

The SWOT analysis is the first stage of planning and will help you make your objectives more specific, for example:

- A strength could be your specialist expertise.
- A weakness could be the lack of a new product.
- An opportunity could be a new or developing market.
- A threat could be a new competitor in your home market.

We've given you a Balancing Risk Worksheet on the next page – just fill in the boxes. It's simple and surprisingly effective in helping you see the 'trees' in the wood!

## SWOT – Stage one

Once you have analysed your potential course of action, assess the importance of each element. Invent your own rating scale. It only needs to be meaningful to you, so could be from −50 to +50, where −50 is very negative and +50 is very positive. For example:

Course of action: Moving jobs

- I will get more opportunity for career progression +30
- I will not enjoy the amount of travelling involved -20

## SWOT – Stage two

Once you've rated each course of action, add up the total for each column and enter it in the 'total' boxes. Then add up the two positive aspects (strengths + opportunities) and put this in the 'total' box of the 'positive' column. Do the same for the negative aspects (weaknesses + threats).

Now, you can see how balanced your decision is by comparing your total 'positive' and 'negative' scores. In other words, do the strengths and opportunities outweigh the weaknesses and threats?

If you have a positive score then congratulations, you seem to have a potentially positive opportunity. However, you will need to make sure that you have really considered whether this is the true picture. Have you fully considered the potential risks and threats? It may be worth reviewing your analysis to make sure. If you have a negative overall balance then this suggests that you have a number of either risks or threats to counter.

Having completed the worksheet, you should have more of an idea of what kind of balance you're achieving. You can use the data in these tables in many different ways; for example:

1. Identifying the 'highs' and 'lows' on the positive and negative indicators, to work out their implications for management issues, team contributions or other work situations.
2. Understanding the strength of your own biases – and planning a strategy to manage them.
3. A starting point for discussions with others about your decision making, and how you could balance your approach.

A word of caution! The SWOT analysis can be very subjective, so don't rely on it alone. It's rare that two people produce the same SWOT analysis of the same situation. Use it as a guide only.

# ● BALANCING RISK WORKSHEET

| Strengths | +/- | Opportunities | +/- |
|-----------|-----|---------------|-----|
|  |  |  |  |
|  |  |  |  |
|  |  |  |  |
|  |  |  |  |
| Total: |  | Total: |  |
| Positive Total: |  |  |  |

| Weaknesses | +/- | Threats | +/- |
|------------|-----|---------|-----|
|  |  |  |  |
|  |  |  |  |
|  |  |  |  |
|  |  |  |  |
| Total: |  | Total: |  |
| Positive Total: |  |  |  |

## ● NEXT STEPS

Having considered the potential biases in your decision making and tried out the exercise above, there are a number of actions that you could take next. These are guidelines and the list is by no means exhaustive.

### Review with others

Review the SWOT analysis with other people – colleagues, team members or your line manager. You could also ask them what they think your biases are!

### Produce a plan to overcome obstacles

Look at the potential 'threats' and 'weaknesses' and produce a plan to counter them. (Consider your 'strengths' and 'opportunities', too, because you may have already identified counter measures in these columns.)

### Look for opportunities to practise

Think about decisions coming up (at work and elsewhere) where you could practise weighing up the risks and benefits. Use the SWOT analysis tool to help you.

## ● FURTHER INFORMATION

If you found this tool useful then you are likely to find the following tools both insightful and relevant:

- How to reframe problems
- How to focus on the bigger picture
- How to make reasoned judgements
- How to be confident in making judgement calls
- How to know when and how to take risks
- How to use optimism to achieve.

## ● REFERENCES

1   Cannon, W. (1929). **Bodily Changes in Pain, Hunger, Fear, and Rage.** New York: Appleton.

2   Poundstone, W. (1992). **Prisoner's Dilemma.** NY: Doubleday.

3   Hastie, R., & Dawes, R. M. (2009). Rational choice in an uncertain world: The psychology of judgement and decision making. SAGE Publications, Incorporated.

4   Kolb, D. (1984). 'Experiential Learning: Experience As The Source Of Learning And Development'. Englewood Cliffs, New Jersey: Prentice-Hall

5   Nicholson, N. (ed.) (1995). Encyclopedic Dictionary of Organizational Behavior. Blackwell.

6   Friesner, T. (2011). **History of SWOT analysis.** Marketing Teacher, 2000-2010.

# INDEX

# ● INDEX

Page numbers in *italic* indicate a graphic or illustration